The *Promise*
of
Bonhoeffer

Also by Benjamin A. Reist

Toward a Theology of Involvement:
The Thought of Ernst Troeltsch

The Promise of Theology
Martin E. Marty, General Editor

The Promise of Barth
The Promise of Bennett
The Promise of Bonhoeffer
The Promise of Buber
The Promise of Bultmann
The Promise of Heschel
The Promise of Kierkegaard
The Promise of H. Richard Niebuhr
The Promise of Reinhold Niebuhr
The Promise of Teilhard de Chardin
The Promise of Tillich

The Promise
of
Bonhoeffer

by
BENJAMIN A. REIST

J. B. LIPPINCOTT COMPANY

Philadelphia and New York

To my parents,
Norman Irvin Reist,
and Ruth Ayrault Reist,
as a token of gratitude

Foreword

In the seventh decade of our century, western Christian thought began to take a basic new turn. Whereas for centuries "world" and "secular" had been seen only negatively, now suddenly they were taken up as positive categories in theology. While the sources and roots for this turn are ancient and deep—certainly they are present in the Bible— no single modern figure did so much to inspire it as the young German theologian Dietrich Bonhoeffer.

What is most remarkable about his feat is that he did it ten years after his death. During his short life he had been regarded as a sort of major-minor scholar and thinker, at home in many topics having to do with faith but no *Wunderkind* or master in any. Philosophy, sociology, ethics, sermonizing, biblical interpretation, and devotional literature were all part of the early Bonhoeffer lore. He was widely read but not necessarily reckoned with. Even his death, in what may have been a "guilty martyrdom" (in Benjamin Reist's phrase) in the last weeks of the Nazi regime, did not give him his permanent place. The Church has a memory filled with martyrs.

Bonhoeffer's *Letters and Papers from Prison,* erratic and half-fulfilled, began to make their impact about ten years after he died. The English translation made them well known in the Anglo-American world. It may well be argued that Bonhoeffer was not needed, that Christian thought was ready to make its move without benefit of a particular figure. But the fact of the matter is that the Church did move along the line of thought that Bonhoeffer had begun to set forth. The phrases and cadences of his "world coming of age" motifs fill recent Christian writing and preaching.

Profound as Bonhoeffer's clue may have been, it left him vulnerable to misinterpreters and casual dismissers. Not a few will feel that they have already coped with and exhausted what he has to offer. Benjamin Reist will provide surprises for them. Bonhoeffer, who dealt so much with the future, still represents promise; in effect, Reist is asking, are we ready for him even now?

MARTIN E. MARTY
The University of Chicago

Preface

To ponder the question of the *promise* of Dietrich Bonhoeffer's thought is to wonder where we should be going now in the light of what he has shown us. This is confusing in Bonhoeffer's case because so much has been said about the striking ideas of his prison writings, with little or no attention to his writings as a whole or to the details of the events in the midst of which he worked.

The latter problem is far more complicated than might be supposed. Of course we have known for years about the broad contours of this unforgettable man's involvement in the mortal struggle against the Third Reich. But we have not had the exacting and meticulous portrayal needed at so many pivotal junctures for the unraveling of his astonishing insights. The appearance of the long-awaited biography by his closest friend and theological comrade, Eberhard Bethge, has changed all this. The details are there for all who will take the time to study them. Those interested in Bonhoeffer's thought have always been indebted beyond measure to Bethge for his endless labors in putting Bonhoeffer's writings before us. Now the crowning achievement is at hand, for now we know the man as well as his thought, and his thought as we know the man, because of the selfless devotion and magnificent scholarship of his friend. It is good news indeed to know that the English translation of the biography is in preparation, so that this remarkable story will soon be available for those who do not handle German. The discerning of the promise of Bonhoeffer's theology is a matter of knowing both his life and his thought.

In this discussion I have had students primarily in mind, both formal and informal students. All references are to the latest paperback editions, where they exist. I have tried to keep my quarrels with the existing translations to an absolute minimum, and have confined all references to the German texts to the notes, where the technically trained can find them if they wish. Even so, on occasion it has been necessary to ponder Bonhoeffer's own words in the text of the discussion.

For those whose study of theological questions may happen to be commencing while reading this volume, let it be said that although Bonhoeffer's thought is rigorously disciplined, and therefore often difficult, nevertheless it is a marvelous place to begin struggling with the gigantic questions that are always both fascinating and terrifying for theology. To follow the decisive turnings of the arguments that drove him to his far horizons is to become well initiated into the demands of theology itself. It is an involvement to which the present can be joyfully welcomed.

BENJAMIN A. REIST

San Anselmo, California
February, 1969

Contents

Abbreviations

Beginning with Chapter II, references to works by Bonhoeffer will be abbreviated as follows:

LP   *Letters and Papers from Prison* (third edition, paperback, 1967)
CF   *Creation and Fall* (paperback edition, 1965)
CD   *The Cost of Discipleship* (paperback edition, 1963)
E   *Ethics* (paperback edition, 1965)
CS   *The Communion of Saints*
AB   *Act and Being*
C   *Christ the Center*

I.

The Man

At dawn on April 9, 1945, Dietrich Bonhoeffer was put to death on the gallows at Flossenbürg in Bavaria, at the hand of a defeated, vindictive, demonic Third Reich. He was two months and five days beyond his thirty-ninth birthday. In that short lifetime, in the midst of the chaos that was the rise and fall of the Nazi state, he had put together theological insights and conclusions, and begun theological labors, that would long remain both controversial and fascinating, perplexing and unavoidable. For some he would epitomize and personify the only way theology *and* the Church can go forward in the twentieth century. For others he would always remain simply an enigma. Who was this man?

The general answer to this question has been known for a long time now. But general answers do not really help when one seeks a penetrating understanding of the life and thought of Dietrich Bonhoeffer. For guesswork must take over all too many crucial junctures. A case of no little cogency can be made for the view that precisely this has limited, if it has not undermined, many of the treatments and interpretations of Bonhoeffer's work that have been appearing with regular frequency over the years. Happily, the guesswork is no longer needed. In 1967 the long-awaited and definitive biography of Bonhoeffer appeared. It is the crowning achievement of the work of his student, then assistant, and closest friend, Eberhard Bethge. Bethge (born in 1909) has devoted his life to putting Bonhoeffer's work before the world of theology. In 1949 he brought out the fragmentary *Ethik*, on which Bonhoeffer worked during the years immediately preceding his arrest (the English translation, *Ethics*, first appeared in 1955). Moreover, Bethge was the recipient of the famous smuggled correspondence from the military prison at Tegel (in Berlin). These letters, plus the letters that Bonhoeffer wrote to his parents from the same prison, formed the basis of *Widerstand und Ergebung* in 1951 (literally, "Resistance and Surrender," published in English translation as *Letters and Papers from Prison*—the initial American edition was entitled *Prisoner for God*—in 1953). Bethge then proceeded to the huge task of editing all of Bonhoeffer's unpublished works, and of writing the biography. On both counts we owe him incalculable debts of gratitude. The biography itself is monumental and massive—it runs to over 1,100 pages in German (an English translation is in preparation). It is also the incisive work of the one who knows better than any other the full range of the life and thought of this unforgettable man. With Bethge's biography before us the sketch of Bonhoeffer's life is both possible and compelling.

The general point can be put simply. Dietrich Bonhoeffer was a highly gifted and promising theologian with an unmistakably deep passion for the concrete life of the Church. Circumstances led to the dominance of the latter dimension. The former concern always remained, but strictly in the context of concreteness. By the late 1930's, 1938 to be exact, he was directly involved in the most radical resistance to Hitler, participating in the efforts to overthrow him. To see why this outcome was both inexorable and an intrinsic part of Bonhoeffer's theological work, we need a detailed etching.

Bonhoeffer's promise as theologian was already apparent in his student days at Tübingen and Berlin. In December of 1927, while he was still twenty-one, he won his graduate degree, the licentiate of theology, with the writing of his dissertation, *Sanctorum Communio* (published in English translation as *The Communion of Saints*), under the celebrated Reinhold Seeberg of Berlin. Two and a half years later, his *Akt und Sein* (English translation, *Act and Being*) won him appointment to the theological faculty at Berlin (as *Privatdozent*, roughly the equivalent of an instructor or lecturer in

[16]

an American university or seminary). Before taking up these duties he spent the academic year 1930–1931 as a student at Union Theological Seminary in New York (where he came to know his closest friend and theological comrade in America, Paul Lehmann, now Auburn Professor of Systematic Theology at Union). Upon his return from the United States he began his lecturing at Berlin with the winter semester of 1931–1932, and continued for two years, through the summer semester of 1933. A group of interested students soon formed around him. His rich promise for a glowing career as a professor of systematic theology was already manifest and under way toward fulfillment.

The events of 1933 interrupted all this, setting in motion an alteration in the form of Bonhoeffer's work that would prove irrevocable. The passion for concreteness became inexorably dominant, leading him to leave the purely academic world behind. Productive theologian he would remain, in the most rigorous sense of the term. But theology in his key would have to be played in the context of the pastoral office in the Confessing Church, that segment of German Protestantism that vigorously resisted Hitler's efforts to control and exploit it.

This concern of Bonhoeffer for the pastoral involvement took shape as early as his promise as theologian. In 1928 he had served as an assistant pastor to a German congregation in Barcelona, Spain. During his year of study at Union close friendship with an American Negro fellow student, Frank Fisher, led him into an astonishingly deep exposure to and identification with the already burgeoning crisis in Black America. When he took up his duties as a teacher at the University of Berlin he maintained this concern for the pastoral involvement. He was ordained in November of 1931, and throughout the winter of 1931–1932 he was responsible for a confirmation class in one of the Berlin slums. In September of 1931 he attended an ecumenical gathering in England, the meeting of the World Alliance at Cambridge, and he returned from that consultation as one of its three Youth

Secretaries, with responsibility for Germany and central Europe.

On January 30, 1933, Adolf Hitler became Chancellor of Germany. By July of the same year the Nazis had accomplished—legally—their initial objective, the establishment of the totalitarian state, with the proclamation of the National Socialist Party as the only legal political party in Germany. July, 1933, also saw the Reichstag's formal recognition of a new "Reich Church," to be led by a "Reich Bishop" whose task it was to unify diverse German Protestantism into a single ecclesiastical organism totally in support of the Third Reich. Vigorous opposition arose immediately. Thus commenced the German Church Struggle. Bonhoeffer was involved in this opposition from the very beginning.

The so-called "German Christians," those who bought Hitler's stratagem for the subjugation of the German Protestant churches and sought to further it, were never completely successful in their efforts. They did succeed in electing the notorious Ludwig Müller as Reich Bishop at the national synod at Wittenberg in September, 1933. But neither Müller nor those who succeeded him in his task (though not in the office of Reich Bishop) were ever able to build the Reich Church that Hitler demanded. At the same time, the opposition was not successful either in the achievements of its goals. The Confessing Church came into existence with the Barmen Declaration of May, 1934. The Barmen Declaration was never adopted by German Protestantism as a whole, or even by a majority of it. And even within the ranks of the Confessing Church itself there was diversity. Bonhoeffer would insist repeatedly that to be a Christian in Germany meant to be a member of the Confessing Church. This put him on the really radical edge of the opposition. Countless men and women suffered for their adherence to the stand of the Confessing Church, and some died for their conviction, but ultimately only a small band saw this opposition to entail what Bonhoeffer argued it must. The last twelve years of his life coincided with the rise and fall of the Third Reich. The development of his theology is unintelligible apart from the story of his role in the German Church Struggle.

Two days after Hitler became Chancellor, Bonhoeffer gave a lecture on the radio entitled "Changes in the Concept of the Leader." In April he wrote an essay on "The Church and the Jewish Question." In August he produced a pamphlet on "The Aryan Paragraph in the Church" (vigorously opposing the German Christians' thesis against converted Jews, by which they sought to exclude from the pastoral office, and indeed from the Church, any Christians of Jewish origin). In September he was hard at work with Martin Niemöller preparing for the development of the Pastors' Emergency League, a milepost on the way to Barmen and beyond. All this suggests that it means to say that from the outset Bonhoeffer was deeply involved in the struggle against the Nazi attempt to take over the Church.

The initial result of Bonhoeffer's role in the opposition will come perhaps as a surprise. He interrupted his teaching at the university and left Germany, to take up the post of pastor to two German congregations in London, the Reformed Church of St. Paul and the German Evangelical Church in Sydenham. This would prove to be the only pastorate he was ever to hold. One could yield to the temptation to construe this as an unambiguously constructive move. The reverse is also possible—one could see it as an evasion of the mounting chaos at home. Neither point would be correct alone. Bonhoeffer, now only twenty-seven years of age, was finding his way into an increasingly darkening future. As Bethge notes, his involvement in the opposition at this stage was strictly a matter of theologically ordered discipline, without the admixture of the drastic political dimension that would later become so decisive.[1] * At any rate, during the two years he spent in this post, Bonhoeffer's ecumenical contacts became much more highly developed, to the point where he became a major interpreter of the German situation to church leaders outside Germany. By late November he had come to know George

* Superior figures refer to the Notes at the end of the text.

Bell, the Bishop of Chichester (1883–1958), who was destined to play a major role in subsequent events. Through Bell, and others high in ecumenical leadership posts, he sought to gain not only recognition of the emerging Confessional Church, but also the explicit acknowledgment of this body as the only authentic Protestant church in Germany. In this connection Bonhoeffer would never be totally successful despite his numerous trips on behalf of ecumenical concerns, and the wide number of celebrated figures with whom he became personally acquainted. However, the individuals whom he touched with the cogency of this argument included impressive people indeed, such as Bishop Bell, and Willem A. Visser 't Hooft, later to become the first General Secretary of the World Council of Churches. Bonhoeffer spent the period from the fall of 1933 to the spring of 1935 in his London pastorate. Though not present, accordingly, at the Synod of Barmen,[2] he nevertheless contributed to the ferment leading up to it with his vigorous and outspoken protest of all that the German Christians sought to impose on the churches of Germany by way of total submission to the Nazi tide.

During the winter of 1935 Bonhoeffer received a decisive summons from the leadership of the Confessing Church. The request was that he return to Germany to undertake the leadership of one of its Preachers' Seminaries. Such institutions had their own checkered past, rooted in the need of the churches to provide for the theological formation of future pastors, as over against the purely academic theological education of the universities. Understandably, as is always the case in theological training, students tended to enjoy the excitement of intellectual discipline more than the regimen leading to the pastoral office itself. An abrupt change in all this came with the swirl of events in the Germany of the 1930's. Initially, the Nazis' targets were simply the church leaders and the university professors. Increasing pressure was brought to bear on such celebrated positions. With the sweeping success of such maneuvers, the Confessing Church turned to the Preachers' Seminaries as the real training ground for its future ministers.

Five of these were established. Bonhoeffer was summoned back from London to assume the direction of one of them, located in Pomerania, first at Zingst, and then at Finkenwalde, near Stettin on the Baltic coast. The challenge was staggering, for already, in effect, such institutions were illegal. Moreover, the assumption of this post cost Bonhoeffer one of his most cherished dreams, a visit to Gandhi in India, which Bishop Bell had helped him to arrange. (We shall comment on this fascinating point later.) Notwithstanding that, Bonhoeffer threw himself into preparations for his new mission, visiting three Anglican monasteries in the process. On April 26, 1935, he began his work at Zingst, with twenty-three students under his guidance, as director and sole teacher. (At this point there were about one hundred seminarians in all in the five seminaries then being operated by the Confessing Church. Characteristically, the staffing of these were one-man operations, under the oversight of Wilhelm Niesel of the Brotherhood Council of the Confessing Church.[3]) Better quarters were found at Finkenwalde, to which the group moved at the end of June, there to remain until it was closed by the Gestapo in September of 1937. (By November of 1937, twenty-seven former Finkenwalde seminarians were under arrest.) This would be one of Bonhoeffer's most productive and far-reaching periods. From this time came two of his most significant books, *Nachfolge* (English translation: *The Cost of Discipleship*), which was published in 1937, and *Gemeinsames Leben* (English translation: *Life Together*), which was put into its final form in 1938. His impression on his students was profound and indelible. One of them was Eberhard Bethge.

In the fall of 1937 the seminary at Finkenwalde was closed by the police. Finkenwalde was at an end, but not the work there begun. In December this work was reorganized, two small groups of students meeting for instruction from Bonhoeffer each week, one at Köslin, a city of 30,000 inhabitants some one hundred miles northeast of Stettin, the other at Schlawe, with a population of 10,000, another twenty miles to the east. This second group met first in Gross-Schlönwitz and then (from April, 1939, on) at Sigurdshof, villages on the edge of Schlawe. In essence, Finkenwalde now existed in dispersion and underground. The cover was provided by the Church Superintendents, Friedrich Onnasch in Köslin and Eduard Block in Schlawe. By their good offices the students were registered as teaching assistants to various pastors in the given cities. However, they lived together, and Bonhoeffer, operating out of Schlawe, spent several days each week with each of the two groups, carrying on the work of instruction along the lines developed at Finkenwalde. In this he was assisted in Köslin by Fritz Onnasch, Superintendent Onnasch's son, and in Gross-Schlönwitz, and later Sigurdshof, by Eberhard Bethge. The ruse worked well, though it brought the hardships of makeshift living conditions and constant traveling between the two locations, and it greatly lengthened the frequent trips Bonhoeffer made to Berlin to get the information he needed to keep up with developments there. But it worked. The Gestapo did not stop this operation until March 15, 1940.

In the summer of 1938 a reunion was held at Zingst (which yielded Bonhoeffer's study on *Temptation*), and in the fall of the same year *Gemeinsames Leben* (*Life Together*), which actually came out of the Finkenwalde experience, was written out in its final form. Early in 1938, however, developments had begun to set in which even the close Finkenwalde circle knew about dimly if at all. What was starting to take shape was Bonhoeffer's involvement in the conspiracy against the Nazi state, into which he was ushered by his brother-in-law, Hans von Dohnanyi.

At this point we must broaden our narrative to include notice of the remarkable family whence Bonhoeffer came. For by no means was his participation in the plot against the Third Reich simply a matter of theology narrowly and romantically conceived. It was deeply rooted, as well, in the matrix that spawned him. Like him, his older brother Klaus and his brothers-in-law Rüdiger Schleicher and Hans von Dohnanyi would die in the fitful spasms that were the death throes of Nazi fascism: Klaus Bonhoeffer and Rüdiger Schleicher at Moabit prison in Berlin, on April 23, 1945, and Hans von Dohnanyi at the concentration camp at Sachsenhausen, on the same day that Dietrich Bonhoeffer was hanged at Flossenbürg, April 9, 1945.

Dietrich Bonhoeffer was born on February 4, 1906, in Breslau. Literally, he was the sixth of eight children, being born minutes ahead of his twin sister, Sabine. His father, Karl, was one of Germany's outstanding psychiatrists, and was professor of neurology and psychiatry at Breslau when Dietrich was born. His mother, Paula, was the granddaughter of a celebrated professor of church history, Karl August von Hase, of Jena. Dietrich was six when, in 1912, his father was called to the University of Berlin. He was raised in the midst of Berlin's academic community, and intellectual and professional pursuits would mark the lives of each of his brothers and sisters as well as himself (except for his older brother, Walter, who died at the front in the First World War). His oldest brother, Karl-Friedrich, became a professor of natural science. The husbands of two of his sisters became professors. And both his brother Klaus and his brother-in-law Hans von Dohnanyi were lawyers. This family as a whole, both by heritage and by concrete action, stood in the midst of that courageous segment of Germany that labored for the reversal of the tragic and demonic course that Hitler charted.

Engrossing as it is, the detailed story of the conspiracy against the Third Reich can hardly be set out even in brief form here.[4] Suffice it to say that it had been brewing virtually from the beginning of Hitler's rise to power. The revulsion that many felt when the true face of the Nazi purpose became apparent with the events of 1933 had to await the commitment of those in high military posts before any real effort to effect a *coup d'état* could be mounted. This was slow in coming, but the events of 1938 at last provided the needed coalescence of effort. Nineteen thirty-eight began with Hitler's deposing of General Freiherr Werner von Fritsch as Commander in Chief of the Army. The manner in which this was carried out (von Fritsch was framed on a homosexual charge) outraged the time-honored Prussian military tradition, and evoked the concerted effort of General Ludwig Beck and others to shape decisive opposition to the entire Nazi enterprise. The following months brought into the open first Hitler's annexation of Austria, and then his move against Czechoslovakia. As Chief of the Army General Staff, General Beck opposed this latter move on military grounds, and in August of 1938 he resigned his post in protest to an intransigence on Hitler's part which he was convinced could lead only to disaster. This paved the way for the *coup* to coincide with Hitler's invasion of Czechoslovakia, Hitler himself to be held for trial before the German people. The debacle at Munich foiled the plan of the conspiracy, since the case against Hitler was predicated on the ruinous portent of any attempted military conquest of Czechoslovakia, and Hitler never had to begin military operations because of the concessions made to him by Prime Minister Neville Chamberlain.

The center of the attempt at a *coup d'état*, as well as of the succeeding efforts to overthrow the Nazis, was in the office of the German Military Intelligence, the *Abwehr*, under Admiral Wilhelm Canaris and his chief assistant, Colonel Hans Oster, both of whom would share the gallows at Flossenbürg with Bonhoeffer. Canaris and Oster provided the skillful leadership that saw to it that the *Abwehr* remained outside the control of Heinrich Himmler and the Gestapo until very late in the war, early 1944 to be exact. Formally the task of the *Abwehr* was counterespionage, and this made it possible for Canaris and Oster to provide an extremely effective protective screen for the resistance to Hitler. By the outbreak of the war in 1939, Canaris's office was the last stronghold of those elements within the military hierarchy who were bent on Hitler's removal, and thus it was in fact the only remaining and durable locus of hope for the conspiracy.

Obviously more than just the military were involved in the work taking place under the cover that Canaris and Oster could provide. The key such figure for our concerns was Hans von Dohnanyi. By 1929 his legal career had led him to an influential post in the Ministry of Justice, in which he continued during the early years of the Third Reich. The contacts he developed made him an invaluable source of information for Bonhoeffer in the latter's own involvement in the German Church Struggle. During these initial years it was quite possible to function with a certain degree of independence inside the judicial establishment, and von Dohnanyi put this to good use, developing from the very outset of the Third Reich a carefully documented and legally exacting record of the criminal offenses of the Nazi enterprise. This loomed up as of tremendous significance for the case being built against Hitler in 1938 by Beck, Canaris, Oster, and those associated with them. From this point on von Dohnanyi worked directly and closely with the group. In August of 1939, in fact, he formally joined the staff of the *Abwehr*, serving as a political expert in Colonel Oster's department, and functioning in a sense as Admiral Canaris's private secretary.[5]

Von Dohnanyi provided Bonhoeffer with his entree into the conspiracy. As Bethge notes, the relationship between them was extremely intimate: "No one . . . stood so close to him in the decisive years as his brother-in-law, Hans von Dohnanyi. From him Bonhoeffer received information, advice, and later on, orders, while he sought in Bonhoeffer ethical certainty and clarifying formulations."[6] Through his brother-in-law, then, Bonhoeffer knew all about the conspiracy in the fateful year 1938, and this at a time when to know about such matters was itself perilous in the extreme. Thus, his involvement in the conspiracy dates from the crisis surrounding the dismissal of General von Fritsch in the opening days of 1938. This initial phase of his involvement was one marked only by collusion and approval, to use Bethge's phrase.[7] The transition from collusion to direct action was not yet at hand. It would not come until after the clearing of his heart and mind which Bonhoeffer experienced during his second, and very brief, trip to the United States in the early summer of 1939.

This second trip to America must be understood with precision. What motivated it primarily was Bonhoeffer's struggle with the issue of pacifism. This dated from his first trip to America. It accounts for his passion to visit Gandhi, whose insight into nonviolent resistance Bonhoeffer longed to grasp at first hand. Now, with the inexorable approach of the resumption of the World War due to the failure of each and every attempt to check Hitler, Bonhoeffer faced the imminent prospect of his own conscription into the German Army. For him this was unthinkable. However, in considering the possibility of conscientious objection he was struggling with far more than his own probable execution. The position itself knew neither legal *nor theological* justification in Germany! Not even his co-laborers in the Confessing Church could be expected to support him. Moreover, were he to take this stand the already tenuous position of the Confessing Church would be even worse, given the record of his role in its work, especially his leadership of the seminary at Finkenwalde. In March of 1939 he went briefly to London, there to seek counsel in his struggle from Bishop Bell, from Visser 't Hooft, from his sister Sabine, and her husband, Professor Gerhard Leibholz (refugees in England from September, 1938, on because of Leibholz's Jewish origin), and from Reinhold Niebuhr of Union Theological Seminary in New York (who was in Great Britain, delivering, in Scotland, his celebrated Gifford lectures, *The Nature and Destiny of Man*). This visit resulted in the efforts of Niebuhr abroad and Paul Lehmann in the United States (who was teaching at Elmhurst College near Chicago) to find a post for Bonhoeffer in America. Immense effort was expended on Bonhoeffer's behalf, especially by Lehmann, to set up the lecture tour and find the ecumenical post in New York that, it was hoped, would lead to an American professorship.

[26]

Understandably, the leadership of the Confessing Church was reluctant to approve Bonhoeffer's departure for America, even for the temporary stay he contemplated. (From the beginning of this entire venture and in the midst of those confusing years, the Americans laboring to extricate Bonhoeffer from Germany were under the mistaken opinion that he would remain permanently in the United States. This was not his own hope. The issue, as we shall see in a moment, was not *whether* he would return home, but *how soon.*) This formal approval was an absolute necessity. Bonhoeffer was already a marked man (for example, his Finkenwalde involvement had led to the formal termination of his faculty status at the University of Berlin in August of 1936), and travel restrictions were being rigorously enforced. The approval was granted. The need of the Confessing Church for teachers of Bonhoeffer's caliber was acute, but his potential for its cause was as great, perhaps greater, outside Germany than was the case, for the moment, at home. On June 2, 1939, he returned to London, and on June 7, in the company of his brother Karl-Friedrich, who was bound for Chicago, there to lecture in physics, he sailed aboard the *Bremen* for the United States.

From his arrival in New York until his abrupt departure on July 7, Bonhoeffer was in residence at Union Theological Seminary (except for a brief visit to President Henry Sloan Coffin's summer residence in Connecticut). While preparing to teach in Union's summer session he wrestled with the problem as it now took shape. The initial offer, from the American side, had been extended under the joint auspices of the Central Bureau of Interchurch Aid and Union Theological Seminary. The idea was that Bonhoeffer would do such teaching as Union could work out for him and at the same time carry on pastoral work with refugees in New York City under the aegis of the ecumenical group sharing the initial appointment. The hope was, again from the American side, that in due time a permanent appointment for Bonhoeffer, either at Union or elsewhere, could be found. From Bonhoeffer's side the dilemma was immediately apparent. A permanent post in the

United States was out of the question, for this meant that he would desert completely his work under the Confessing Church in Germany. Obviously his assumption of a pastoral post with refugees would jeopardize his return. Moreover, were he to accept this post he would remove the possibility for someone to undertake it whose return to Germany might already be blocked. The worsening news from home combined with this turmoil to force Bonhoeffer's final decision, which he reached after hours of pacing a humid Times Square on the evening of June 19. Subsequent word from Karl-Friedrich that he was returning to Germany following his own refusal of the professorship offered him in Chicago confirmed the decision all the more. The correspondence and diary from these days show the depth and portent of the conclusion Bonhoeffer had reached. The most incisive indication is in the letter he wrote to Niebuhr at the beginning of July:

> . . . sitting here in Dr. Coffin's garden I have had the time to think and to pray about my situation and that of my nation and to have God's will for me clarified. I have come to the conclusion that I have made a mistake in coming to America. I must live through this difficult period of our national history with the Christian people of Germany. I will have no right to participate in the reconstruction of Christian life in Germany after the war if I do not share the trials of this time with my people. My brothers in the Confessional Synod wanted me to go. They may have been right in urging me to go; but I was wrong in going. Such a decision each man must make for himself. Christians in Germany will face the terrible alternative of either willing the defeat of their nation in order that Christian civilization may survive, or willing the victory of their nation and thereby destroying our civilization. I know which of these alternatives I must choose; but I cannot make that choice in security . . . .[8]

On July 6, Paul Lehmann came to New York in a last effort to dissuade him. Failing that, Lehmann saw him off at midnight, July 7. On July 27, after a ten-day stop in London, Bonhoeffer returned to Berlin. Four years of a double life, as Bethge puts it,[9] remained, followed by two years in prison, and the gallows.

Upon his return Bonhoeffer resumed his work with the students at Köslin and, now, Sigurdshof. At the same time his contacts with the conspiracy, through von Dohnanyi, increased. With the outbreak of the war in September of 1939 two developments brought new hope to the circle operating out of the *Abwehr*. The capitulation of Poland paved the way for preparations for the march through the Netherlands and Belgium, and thus the drastic extension of the proportions of the war was no longer a matter of debate. Second, the conspiracy received the details of Nazi atrocities in Poland. The case against Hitler before Munich was now all the more cogent. General Beck urged von Dohnanyi to bring his *Skandalchronik* up to date, and a way was now sought to effect what had misfired when the opportunity afforded a year earlier in the Czechoslovakian crisis disappeared. At this time Bonhoeffer met Colonel Oster and shared with him the struggle of resolution, that what was treason in the eyes of the nation was the only true love of country.[10] At this time, too, Bonhoeffer began work on his *Ethics*, which had long been taking shape as his major theological task, and which now received urgent stimulus and radical extension from the activities into which he was being irrevocably drawn.

In March of 1940, as we have noted, Köslin and Sigurdshof were closed by the Gestapo. Such contact as Bonhoeffer now had with those of his students not under arrest or in the army was fluid and diffuse, correspondence and occasional visits providing the only means of maintaining contact. From this point until his arrest his life oscillated between his theological work and these continued contacts, on the one hand, and the rising tempo of his direct activities in the conspiracy, on the other. "Double life" is anything but a merely rhetorical metaphor. The spring of 1940 was spent in Berlin, the summer saw three visits to East Prussia. Late in the summer Oster and von Dohnanyi proposed that he take a post in the *Abwehr* himself, thus to be placed beyond the reach of conscription into the army, and thus to facilitate the conspiracy's use of his ecumenical contacts. At the same time the pressure from the side of the Gestapo was incessant. In September of 1940 he was forbidden to speak in public, and to publish his writings, and ordered to report to the police. Through September and October he worked on his *Ethics* at Klein-Krössin, an estate near Stettin about which we shall have more to say later. At the end of October, now formally a counterespionage agent of the German Military Intelligence (!), he was dispatched to the *Abwehr* office in Munich. Josef Müller, a leading Munich lawyer and devout Catholic, and in a sense Bonhoeffer's Catholic counterpart in the conspiracy, as we shall see, secured hospitality for him at the Benedictine monastery at Ettal (near Munich). He arrived there on November 17, 1940, and stayed through February of 1941. The bulk of his time was devoted to the *Ethics*. This proved to be the longest uninterrupted period he would be able to give to it.

With the outbreak of the war the task of the conspiracy was rendered far more complicated than had been the case with the abortive attempt in the days before Munich. Now, direct contact with the Allied governments was an urgent and dangerous necessity. Everything depended not only on a successful *coup d'état* but also on Allied recognition of the government that would replace the Nazi establishment, and the willingness of the Allies to negotiate peace with this government. This is where Bonhoeffer's major role in the plot focused. Equipped with the necessary papers to get him across the border he traveled as a courier, supposedly on missions for German counterespionage, but actually to get the word of the conspiracy to the governments of the Allies, particularly Great Britain, through ecumenical channels. The necessity for the assurance that the *coup* would be supported was far more urgent than may be apparent at first glance. Certainly one of the many factors accounting for the rise of Hitler in the first place was Germany's almost universally disquieted bitterness over the Versailles settlement at the end of the

First World War. The Generals on whom the success of the attempt had depended from the beginning could not be expected to take the staggering risks involved without the solid assurance that Versailles would not be repeated. Josef Müller's role had been similar to Bonhoeffer's now, though it had unfolded earlier, in October of 1940, with the attempt to gain contact with and agreement from the British by way of the Vatican. Bonhoeffer's missions commenced in the spring of 1941. Clearly, more than simply the forwarding of information was involved. What he was actually engaged in was clandestine diplomacy.

In all, Bonhoeffer made six trips outside Germany on behalf of the conspiracy: the first two to Switzerland (February 24–March 24, 1941 and August 28–September 26, 1941), the third to Norway (April 10–18, 1942), the fourth to Switzerland again (May 12–23, 1942), the fifth to Sweden (May 30–June 2, 1942), and the last to Italy (June 26–July 10, 1942). The last three are perhaps the most significant. Bonhoeffer learned in Switzerland that Bishop Bell was in Sweden, and that his trip would officially end on June 2. This led to hasty preparations in the *Abwehr* to get Bonhoeffer to Stockholm, for the opportunity at hand must not be missed. Canaris was able to get him an official Courier-Passport from the foreign office, which was issued at dawn on May 30, and that same day he flew to Stockholm.

The details of this mission are fascinating indeed. Bell was astonished to see Bonhoeffer. Bonhoeffer was even more surprised, and no doubt unnerved, to find that Dr. Hans Schönfeld had also come from Geneva to see Bell. Schönfeld and Bonhoeffer had the same purpose, but Schönfeld, posted in Geneva throughout the war by the German Evangelical Church (*not* the Confessing Church), moved in a different circle and at a different level from what was the case with the group operating out of the *Abwehr*. However all that may be, Bonhoeffer disclosed to Bell the full particulars of the conspiracy, including the names of the key figures involved, for relay to the British Foreign Office. A code was devised for Bell to use in cabling his findings, either by way of Sweden, or by way of Visser 't Hooft in Geneva. Upon his return to England, Bishop Bell persisted in a determined effort to persuade Anthony Eden, and others, that a positive response must go to the conspiracy. This was not forthcoming, however, for the Allied policy of unconditional surrender was already crystallized.[11] In late July, Bell cabled to this effect to Visser 't Hooft. Meanwhile von Dohnanyi and Bonhoeffer went to Italy, ultimately to Rome, to see if word of a favorable decision from the British might be materializing through the Vatican channels Josef Müller had prepared.

In setting out these brief details of the encounter with Bishop Bell in Sweden we have glimpsed the main picture of Bonhoeffer's work for the conspiracy. He had other tasks to perform, participating in the conversations and preparing initial drafts envisioning the new government that, it was hoped, was to follow the *coup*. Such activity plus the continuation of reflection and writing on the *Ethics* whenever possible accounts for the periods between the missions noted above. This was not all that occupied his attention, though. On January 17, 1943, he was engaged to be married to Maria von Wedemeyer, then eighteen years of age. He had known her since she was twelve. Her grandmother, Ruth von Kleist-Retzow of Stettin, was a remarkable person, deeply involved in the cause of the Confessing Church, and a major supporter of the effort at Finkenwalde.[12] As a child, Maria von Wedemeyer often attended Sunday services at Finkenwalde with her grandmother, and as she herself tells us, she first met Bonhoeffer in connection with the confirmation class he conducted for her brother and two cousins.[13] The Kleist estate at Klein-Krössin was one of the recurrent places of refuge and residence for Bonhoeffer during these unsettled years. He was there in September and October of 1940 working on the *Ethics*. In December of 1941 he convalesced there following a bout with pneumonia. He was there again in June of 1942, between the trips to Sweden and Italy, and on this occasion saw Maria there on a visit from her home in Pätzig. It was then that they resolved to be married. Their plans were interrupted by the arrest that spring from which Bonhoeffer would never return. His youthful fiancée, however, played a large role in the difficult years remaining for him. Her visits, her correspondence, and the hopes they shared for the future were major sources of the courage on which he daily depended.

The warning was sounded in the fall of 1942, and from this point on the conspirators knew that time was short. In October an *Abwehr* agent from Munich, named Schmidhuber, was arrested for taking foreign currency across the border to Jewish refugees whom the conspiracy had got into Switzerland. He talked, and the Gestapo learned something of the work of Oster and von Dohnanyi and of the trips of Josef Müller (to the Vatican) and Bonhoeffer (to Sweden). These were now being watched closely, though Himmler's men did not yet realize the full extent of what they were trailing. *Their* concern was to get at Canaris and thus remove the military intelligence agency from the control of the army to the control of the Gestapo. On April 5, 1943, they moved, arresting Hans and Christine von Dohnanyi, Josef Müller and his wife, and Bonhoeffer. At the same time Oster was forced to resign from the *Abwehr* and placed under house arrest. Unwittingly, the Gestapo had struck at the heart of the conspiracy. Himmler's men did not know that two attempts on Hitler's life had failed in the preceding month. On March 13 two time bombs, which Canaris, von Dohnanyi, and General Lahousen of the *Abwehr* staff had flown to Smolensk, were placed aboard the plane on which Hitler returned from the eastern front. The bombs failed to explode. And on March 21 a similar attempt to take the lives of Hitler, Goering, Himmler, and Keitel (at the cost of the life of Colonel Freiherr von Gersdorff, who carried two bombs in his overcoat) failed because of a last-minute change in Hitler's schedule. That the *Abwehr* was indeed the center of massive activity against the Third Reich did not come into the open until the investigations following the failure of Count Klaus von Stauffenberg's celebrated attempt on Hitler's life at Rastenburg in East Prussia, on July

20, 1944. These investigations turned on the Gestapo's /discovery, on September 22, of the *Abwehr's* secret documents, including von Dohnanyi's *Skandalchronik*, at Zossen.[14]

Bonhoeffer was first taken to the military prison at Tegel in Berlin. He was a counterespionage agent under suspicion, and thus under the jurisdiction of the military courts. He had one last service to perform for the conspiracy, and that was to keep quiet—or rather, so to deceive his interrogators that those still outside could carry the resistance forward. In this he was confronted with precisely the same task as von Dohnanyi and Müller. (They were not in Tegel, but in another military prison in Berlin, one reserved for prisoners with officer's rank.) Of the three only Müller survived the holocaust at the end. All three, though, were successful in misleading their questioners. From the outset the investigation seemed to be, and in fact was, endless. For the prosecutors the key figure was von Dohnanyi, not Bonhoeffer, and the target was the *Abwehr*, and neither von Dohnanyi, Müller, nor Bonhoeffer in themselves. Moreover, a prolonged illness on von Dohnanyi's part slowed proceedings even more. Throughout the long period of delay and endless uncertainty, from the day of his arrest to the shattering failure of July 20, 1944, when hope waned, Bonhoeffer knew the frustration, the torment, the trial of life in a Nazi prison, intensified by anxiety over the possibility of a similar fate for his family and his fiancée. At the time only the close circle of the family, together with Bethge (who married Bonhoeffer's niece, Renate Schleicher, later that spring), Maria von Wedemeyer, who came to live with his parents in order to be closer, and a few others, knew of his whereabouts and his struggle. For his colleagues in the Confessing Church he had simply dropped out of sight.

However difficult the time at Tegel was, it was not one of stagnation. Fairly regular visits from his family and fiancée were possible, and they were able to supply him with basic necessities of life, and, above all, the books he requested. Early in the imprisonment he was permitted to write his family—a one-page letter every four days. These he alternated between his parents and his fiancée. They passed through the hands of his prosecutor as a matter of course. Six months into the time at Tegel his contacts with guards and medical orderlies were such that he was able to begin the fairly extensive correspondence by which his last reflections have come to us. This material, sent mainly to Bethge, was smuggled out and thus not written with the prison censors in mind, though obviously much was said in a guarded way. Bethge tells us that these letters were "Bonhoeffer's elixir of life in Tegel." [15] They are the famous *Letters and Papers from Prison*, whose impact on the world of theology has proved to be permanent. As we shall see, this volume consists mainly of the letters to his parents and to Bethge from his lonely Tegel cell. The letters to his fiancée have not been published, though her article, "The Other Letters from Prison" (1967) provides an invaluable insight into the thought and hopes of those dark days.[16] The *Letters and Papers from Prison* and the *Ethics*, both posthumously published by Bethge, set out the farthest reaches of Bonhoeffer's theological work.

The discovery of the *Abwehr's* secret documents at Zossen in September of 1944 brought even this kind of creativity to a sharp halt. On October 8, Bonhoeffer, now conclusively and deeply implicated in the plot, was moved from Tegel to the notorious prison at Prinz-Albrecht-Strasse, the Berlin headquarters of the Gestapo. Here he would see something again of von Dohnanyi and Müller. Here also he came into contact with the British officer Payne Best (of the celebrated Venlo incident), whose account of Bonhoeffer's last days was one of the earliest indications of what finally took place. On February 7, he was taken to the concentration camp at Buchenwald, where he shared a cell with General von Rabenau, and his immediate circle of fellow prisoners included General von Falkenhausen; the British officers Payne Best and Hugh Falconer; a Russian pilot and nephew of Molotov, Wassili Kokorin; Josef Müller; Captain Ludwig Gehre, one of Oster's colleagues in the *Abwehr*; and others equally noteworthy.

Bonhoeffer was now numbered among the most prized

prisoners of the closing days of the Third Reich. Some of these, such as Josef Müller, would escape and survive. Some were high figures who were perhaps being held as possible pawns in a fitful last negotiation with the now invincible Allies (such as Count von Schuschnigg, the former Chancellor of Austria, and Martin Niemöller, who was being held at Dachau). In the last days many would be released and simply left for the advancing Allied armies to find. Some, though, especially those directly related to the heart of the conspiracy, were marked for certain death by Hitler and Himmler themselves.

On April 3, late in the evening, Bonhoeffer and fifteen other prisoners were taken south from Buchenwald. A tense moment occurred when the truck stopped at Weiden (north of Regensburg) where the turn to the left toward the extermination camp at Flossenbürg could mean only one thing. The truck continued on to Regensburg, though it was soon stopped, and Müller, Gehre, and one other were removed. Bonhoeffer was overlooked. From this point on he and the others felt that perhaps new hope of release was real. After the night in the prison at Regensburg the group continued, now up the Danube, and, turning north again, to the little forest village of Schönberg (south of Zweisel), there to be held in the village schoolhouse. For Bonhoeffer, that last hope that had emerged as the truck moved beyond the Flossenbürg turn-off at Weiden now disappeared. The court-martial hastily taking shape at Flossenbürg located him and brought him to the extermination camp. There he was tried late on the night of April 8, along with Canaris, Oster, Dr. Karl Sack, the chief army judge who had been in the *Abwehr* conspiracy from the beginning, and two members of Oster's staff, Dr. Theodor Strunck, a lawyer, and Captain Gehre. At dawn on Monday, April 9, these six went to the gallows together. Within days the American Army moved through Flossenbürg. A month later the Third Reich was at an end.

(To complete the record: The convener of the court-martial

at Flossenbürg on April 8 had presided at the court-martial on the preceding day which condemned Hans von Dohnanyi, who also was executed on April 9, at Sachsenhausen. Klaus Bonhoeffer and Rüdiger Schleicher were among those murdered by the Gestapo at Moabit prison in Berlin two weeks later, on April 23.)

Simply the recounting of Bonhoeffer's life in somewhat detailed perspective is enough to suggest that events provide the clues to his theology. This is true in fact of everyone, but nowhere perhaps is it so graphically the case as here. No penetrating treatment of Bonhoeffer's ideas can ever take place without an exacting understanding of the turbulence through which he lived and died. This is absolutely crucial for any worthy effort to come to terms with his thought. Of necessity the closing phase of his theological work yielded fragmentary projections of the themes to which he hoped, one day, to devote concentrated scholarly effort. This is clearly the case with the *Letters and Papers from Prison*. It is no less true of the *Ethics*. Bethge insists in introducing this latter work that we do not have the book Bonhoeffer wanted to write, but only the initial studies on which it would be based.[17] Accordingly, any discussion of formulations from either of these must move out of a grasp of the development of these ideas. Any other procedure *must* be wrong, and simply cannot be regarded as responsible. Before one can deal with the portent of his work, with the direction he suggested for theology to follow, one must be clear not on what he might have meant but on what he did say. The arresting question for us does not concern what he was looking for but what he did see! However, to put the question this way is to make absolutely necessary the careful indication of the decisive contours of his involvement. In the light of what we now have before us these are such that any isolated attention to his ideas, even though these might be treated with rigorous concern for their sweeping development, is not enough. To discuss Bonhoeffer's thought is not simply a matter of the history of ideas, it is a matter of the history of a man and his times. At least five crucial observations are in order in this connection.

(1) First of all we must emphasize what Bethge calls the "two turning points along [Bonhoeffer's] way." [18] This is developed on a grand scale in the biography, and it is epitomized in a succinct article Bethge prepared for publication in the fall of 1967. In the latter he formulates the matter this way: "The first [turning point] may have occurred about 1931–32 and might be formulated thus: Dietrich Bonhoeffer the theologian became a Christian. The second began in 1939: Dietrich Bonhoeffer the Christian became a contemporary, a man of his own particular time and place. . . . The sequence is what matters and the combination is rare." [19] "Theologian, Christian, Contemporary" (the subtitle of the biography)— in that order, and in a progression that did not exclude the prior phase in each instance, but, rather, transmuted it into a more profound, more drastic, more far-reaching import—this is the structure of the development of Bonhoeffer's life. It is also the clue to the uniqueness of his impact on all who take him seriously. The rigorous theological training to which he responded in his student days yielded a youthful potential with all the tools needed for a lasting contribution as a theologian. The taking up of responsibility as teacher and pastor added to this an urgency of commitment and concern that, given the events of 1933 and beyond, removed all traces of academic aloofness. As Bethge puts it in an incisive comment, Bonhoeffer was a theologian who became a preacher.[20] This in turn thrust him into an unreserved involvement in the awful events of his time. The Christian became an authentic contemporary, totally identified with his co-laborers, in direct correlation with all that swirled around him—identified on their terms, not his own, and yet maintaining his own identity in the midst of it all.[21] The one word that cannot be used with reference to Bonhoeffer is "detached." The one word that cannot be avoided in reflecting on his life is "involved."

(2) In clarifying the point just noted, Bethge comments,

"in the year 1932 he found his calling, in 1939, his destiny." [22] We have seen what this entailed. In reflecting on it we must reckon with a fact that is puzzling at first. Bonhoeffer has had an astonishing impact on Americans, both because of his martyrdom and because of his ideas. But one looks in vain for a parallel impact in Germany. There many regarded him, and still do, as a political martyr, even a traitor, and thus anything but a truly Christian witness.[23] The result is that his theological work has received a wider hearing outside Germany than it has in his homeland. And this is not restricted to the American scene, nor to the English-speaking theological world. An East German theologian, Hanfried Müller, in an impressive argument in 1961, *Von der Kirche zur Welt* (From the Church to the World), "makes him all but a Marxist, or at least, the great Christian apostle to the Marxists," as Paul Lehmann observes.[24]

Why this sharp difference? Why is it not the same inside Germany as outside? American readers are likely to oversimplify this, and thus miss the decisive question in the destiny he risked in the late 1930's. One of the most memorable rewards of working through Bethge's gigantic biography is the clarification of this decisive issue. Bethge distinguishes five levels of the German opposition to the Nazis: (1) passive resistance—there were those who simply refused to cooperate, but nothing more; (2) open ideological opposition—those who forcefully articulated their opposition, but whose articulation did not include the conceptualization of a new political future (an example would be Martin Niemöller); (3) complicity with *preparations* for revolution—notably on the part of high church officers (e.g., Hanns Lilje); (4) active preparation for the future of a post-Nazi Germany (e.g., Helmut von Moltke); and (5) direct involvement in the conspiracy against the Third Reich.[25]

One could, and some did, die at the hands of the Nazis for their involvement at any one of the levels of resistance, including the first. Bonhoeffer, however, was one of the very few, not quite but nearly alone, who moved to the fifth level of resistance on theological grounds. Striking though it may seem, even more was at stake than simply the risk of his own life. He was moving against the stream of classical Lutheran theology, for which such *political* activity was—and is—highly suspect in a particular way. The issue, then and now, was not simply that an assassin's plot was of necessity involved. The issue was, rather, that for men like Bonhoeffer the *political* order had a *positive theological significance.* As churchmen moved down these levels of resistance this problem intensified. Not only personal risk increased with each new stage, but also an unnerving loneliness—the loneliness accompanying the movement beyond a theological tradition with no precedents for such activity. Bonhoeffer is a major figure in breaking new trails on this question, as we shall see later. But inside Germany, then and now, and outside Germany, both in the West and in the East, he was striking for new frontiers, beyond which only those who either did or can move as far as he did can go.

(3) In dealing with the life and thought of Bonhoeffer we are confronted with the most fascinating and terrifying yield of Christian faith. We are reckoning with a *guilty martyr*. Twice in the biography, and at the pivotal point of the epitomizing essay, Bethge calls our attention to the striking passage whence the phrase comes: "A mutation was beginning which Bonhoeffer once, in 1932, predicted, when—without fully realizing its implications and its real shape—he said that the blood of the martyrs might once again be demanded, but 'this blood, if we really have the courage and loyalty to shed it, will not be innocent, shining like that of the first witnesses for the faith. On our blood lies heavy guilt, the guilt of the unprofitable servant who is cast into outer darkness.' " [26]

The depths of this point defy superficial handling, and knowledge of this matter may dispel once and for all the sentimentality that can undermine any real struggle with Bonhoeffer's theological legacy. His course would demand the living out of these lines from a 1932 sermon. Without doubt this is what troubled him as he wrestled with decision as to whether he should remain in America in the summer of 1939. When he wrote to Niebuhr he meant it—his choice would not be made in security. He already knew explicitly what he was returning to Germany to do. What was involved was not a simple stand against a maniacal tyrant. What was involved was "the sacrifice of Christian reputation," [27] in the most basic and elemental sense of the term. Paul Schneider is the name of a pastor who died in 1939 at the hands of the Gestapo for the simple refusal to obey an order (in a sense, level 1 above). He is rightly regarded as a martyr, and this his crown was earned in a way that must humble all who know of it. But what he did and what awaited Bonhoeffer are different in kind, not degree. Bonhoeffer's gallows was in one demonic sense legally correct. *This* is what he was moving toward in the years leading up to his participation in the conspiracy. With fear and trembling we must note the awful contrast of these two sacrifices. We must see that *guilty* martyrdom leaves its own deep mark, makes its own witness, and uniquely binds Christians to men of all persuasions with the challenge of unflinching, uncontrolled, common involvement. Thus, awesome to behold, it costs more.

(4) We must be careful to note that this guilty martyrdom of which we have just spoken had to do with the conspiracy against the Third Reich. It would be extremely misleading to think of this as having its only focus in the plot on Hitler's life. Bonhoeffer did not write the *Ethics* and he did not struggle with his prison writings in order to develop a theological rationale for murder. What did take place was a theologically informed involvement in the most perilous of all ventures in Nazi Germany—the attempt at a *coup d'état*. That this could and probably would entail the attempted tyrannicide was clear from the beginning, and Bonhoeffer did not shrink from the implication. However, it is the broader picture of the whole terrain of the hopes of that circle in the *Abwehr* that must be continually kept in mind. This is not to suggest that we should ignore the extreme to which the conspiracy would go, or that we should pretend that the transition from complicity to direct and active participation did not leave its deep mark on Bonhoeffer's thought. But it is to sug-

gest that the culmination of his life and work was not the result of a myopic fixation on a single problem or cluster of problems.

Bonhoeffer's theology will always be of cardinal significance for those who must live through revolutionary times, not because he was a ruthless revolutionary, but because he could not stand aside while a world was dying. The risks that he willingly shared were the risks that always attend the hard collision of one way of ordering the life of man with another. Such concreteness is always marked by the almost unavoidable possibility of error, even of guilt. This, though, is the characteristic mark of a theology that cannot avoid but, rather, must embrace the problems of the world.

(5) The refusal to stand aside—we dare not leave it at this. Bonhoeffer not only refused to stand aside, he built on the refusal, he struggled with the constructive tasks that alone can give such refusals authenticity and meaning. Primarily this was because he could do no other, given his faith in Christ. Christology is that part of theology concerned with the uniqueness and significance of Jesus Christ. For Bonhoeffer, involvement in the world, and thus participation in the conspiracy, was a christological matter. Presently we shall be seeing how this permeates all that he wrote from beginning to end. But already we have seen enough to know that the genius of his Christology had to do with the fact that concreteness and Christian faith are intimately related—they are in fact two sides of the same coin.

There is a famous remark from the days at Tegel, made by Bonhoeffer to a fellow prisoner, an Italian professor named Gaetano Latmiral. It epitomizes his understanding of how he, a Christian pastor, could take the active role in the conspiracy that he had. As Latmiral recalls it, Bonhoeffer said "that he as Pastor did not only have the duty to console the victims of a mad man who drove a speeding car down a crowded street, but that he must also try to stop him." [28] That is typical of one for whom theology and context are never separable. We must now turn to his theology itself, and seek to discern the promise it holds for us.

II.

Conclusions along the Way

One of the last letters that we have from Bonhoeffer's cell at Tegel contains the outline of a book that he hoped to write. All we have is a sketch of what he proposed to do in this discussion, and to this sketch we will be returning in a later chapter. The words introducing the sketch, though, are worth pondering as we begin looking directly at Bonhoeffer's ideas: "We must move out again into the open air of intellectual discussion with the world, and risk saying controversial things, if we are to get down to the serious problems of life. I feel obliged to tackle these questions as one who, although a 'modern' theologian, is still aware of the debt that he owes to liberal theology" (LP 200).

To be sure, the "controversial things" to which he is referring here are pointed to in the memorable phrases of his prison writings. The book he is proposing would be brief of necessity, given the context in which he worked, but even so it would entail a systematic articulation of the ideas with which he was experimenting. The fact is, however, that Bonhoeffer had been saying "controversial things" from the very beginning of his theological work. The incisive clue as to why this is actually the case comes from his own hand, and is contained in the second sentence of this citation. To see this, one must know what Bonhoeffer meant by " 'modern' theologian" and "liberal theology."

It was at the hands of the latter that he had been trained. Liberal theology had its beginnings with the work of Friedrich Schleiermacher (1768–1834), a gigantic figure who is rightly regarded as the father of modern Protestant theology. Schleiermacher's influence was massive. The line of development emanating from him contained deep variations and radical alterations, but in one way or another these are all traceable to the ferment he began. Sometimes called "nineteenth-century theology," this tradition ended, or, better, went into eclipse, not with the calendar change to the twentieth century, but with the years during and immediately following the First World War. In the 1920's, then, it was on the wane, though it was vibrant and brilliant still, especially at the hands of two of Bonhoeffer's teachers in Berlin, Adolf von Harnack and Reinhold Seeberg. (Ernst Troeltsch, who also taught at Berlin from 1915 on and whose thought had a deep impact on Bonhoeffer, died early in 1923, the year before Bonhoeffer commenced his studies at Berlin, following his year at Tübingen.)

The 1920's saw a revolution within Protestant theology, entailing a radical critique of the entire line from Schleiermacher forward, and both charting new beginnings and envisioning new horizons for the theological enterprise as a whole. The key figure in this abrupt change was Karl Barth (1886–1968), though by no means was the new mood confined to him. Several others of equal stature must be mentioned as well whenever this point is under consideration— figures such as Emil Brunner, Friedrich Gogarten, Paul Tillich, Rudolf Bultmann, and, in America, Reinhold Niebuhr. This list is not exhaustive, but it may serve to suggest that here we are not dealing with the work or influence of one man. It was to these figures, and those who moved with them, that Bonhoeffer was pointing when he used the phrase " 'modern' theologian" in the passage before us.

Bonhoeffer will always symbolize the fact that Protestant theology in the modern world has its roots in *both* of these periods of development. Indeed, he may well personify what happens when they are authentically combined. In typically Germanic style the proponents of the new mood of the 1920's and the defenders of an old theological liberalism were ranged in sharply controversial debates. In the midst of these Bonhoeffer cut his theological teeth. Already in his earliest works, the dissertation, *Sanctorum Communio* (*The Communion of Saints*), and the discussion qualifying him for appointment to the Berlin faculty, *Akt und Sein* (*Act and Being*), he put together arguments that defied the easy critique of either side of the regnant disputes. Intellectual independence marked his theological creativity, and this was rooted in a rare combination: training by the old liberals plus perceptive sensitivity to the concerns that called them into question. From beginning to end he worked as one of the really few members of a new theological generation who carried into the realm of constructive efforts the rich heritage he had gained from the older liberal tradition. Accordingly, a phony synthesis of the old with the more recent was hardly his goal. Rather, both because of the terrible years in which he lived and because of his own creativity, he forged truly new concepts, and put these to work in ways that have evoked the consternation of theological ideologists of either the past or the more recent traditions. It will be of real help for our own understanding of his thought if we pause to clarify this.

According to Bethge, Reinhold Seeberg, under whom Bonhoeffer did his dissertation, left three indelible marks on Bonhoeffer's thinking. First, he taught him that the traditional "theological loci" were arbitrary. That is to say, theology *can* discuss its basic concerns under the traditional headings (e.g., Creation, Trinity, Original Sin, etc.), but it does not have to unless it so wishes. Second, Bonhoeffer learned from Seeberg the hostility toward metaphysics with which Albrecht Ritschl marked those whom he taught. (Ritschl was the key figure between Schleiermacher and the time of Seeberg and his generation.) Third, it was from Seeberg that Bonhoeffer learned "to take the category of the social seriously." Indeed, Bonhoeffer would go his teacher one better in this connection. Seeberg saw the social, along with the historical, as an "essential characteristic of man." Bonhoeffer sharpened this in his view that the social must be "the essential characteristic of all theological concepts." [1] All of these points, particularly the last, are crucial for any attempt to deal with Bonhoeffer's thought. Something of the secret of the vigor and the clarity of his ideas is before us here.

At the same time we must take note of the impact of Barth's thought on Bonhoeffer.[2] Barth's celebrated commentary on Romans (1st edition, 1919; 2nd edition, 1922) triggered the ferment that led to the radical change in the Protestant theological conversation, bringing the emergence of so-called neo-orthodoxy, as it was termed in those early days. This brought Barth from his pastorate in a small Swiss village into signal prominence, and to the series of professorships in which he has left his deep mark on theology, first at Göttingen (1921), then Münster (1925), then Bonn (1930), finally, Basel (from 1935, when the Nazis expelled him from Germany, until his retirement). From the commentary forward Barth has had one mighty theme, Christology. His voluminous writings received their permanent form when, after an initial and tentative start in 1927, he commenced work on his gigantic, multivolumed *Church Dogmatics* in 1932. This entailed the attempt to think through and articulate the entire range of Christian doctrine with direct and explicit reference to Jesus Christ.

In his own student days Bonhoeffer drank deeply from Barth's writings. Both *The Communion of Saints* and *Act and Being* clearly manifest this. His first meeting with Barth occurred when, in the summer of 1931, he spent three weeks with him at Bonn upon his return from the year at Union Theological Seminary. (This had been arranged by a fellow student at Union, Erwin Sutz of Switzerland, who was to remain one of Bonhoeffer's close friends.) They were then associated in the German Church Struggle (Barth played *the* major theological role at Barmen), and later, during Bonhoeffer's trips for the conspiracy, they would meet again in Basel. This relationship had its tense moments. Barth, for example, was mystified when Bonhoeffer took the post in London in 1933. And Bonhoeffer moved to his own trenchant critique of Barth's theology in the midst of his reflections at Tegel, as we shall see. Nevertheless, it was the role of Barth's theology to intensify Bonhoeffer's own articulation of the fact that Christology is the heart of the entire theological enterprise, and this added the decisive emphasis in which the liberal tradition that trained him was defective.

Before leaving this matter three observations should be noted. First, Barth did not know Bonhoeffer's work in detail until after the latter's death, and it is an open question as to whether he ever took the farthest reaches of Bonhoeffer's efforts seriously. Second, the Barth that Bonhoeffer knew had much of his major work yet before him when Bonhoeffer died. Bonhoeffer knew the *Church Dogmatics* only through volume II/2, and that volume he read in prison. Third, Bonhoeffer was never Barth's *student*, and this is of the utmost significance. In spite of himself, Barth could and did produce disciples and a school of thought. Bonhoeffer was never touched by Barth in this way. Throughout the matter of Barth's influence on him one beholds Bonhoeffer being very much his own man. This accounts for the independence of his own insistence that theology's main business is clarifying the uniqueness and the significance of Jesus Christ.

Against the background of this cluster of observations the cogency of reading Bonhoeffer's work as a whole in the light of the remark from Tegel with which we began this chapter is beyond debate. The question for us now becomes this: What is the lasting yield of the work of this "modern" theologian who was aware of his debt to liberal theology? For our initial look we shall ponder two key arguments. The first is from lectures that he gave during the winter semester of 1932–1933 at Berlin, and subsequently published in 1933 under the title *Schöpfung und Fall* (English translation: *Creation and Fall*). The second is from *Nachfolge* (English translation: *The Cost of Discipleship*), the great work from the Finkenwalde days, published in November of 1937, and the book by which he was best known during his lifetime. In so doing we are deliberately leaving on the table *The Communion of Saints* and *Act and Being*. This is not because they are unimportant. It is, rather, because in these early writings, as Bethge notes, "he had still spoken in foreign tongues and with borrowed ideas which makes them such difficult reading." [3] To appraise the promise of Bonhoeffer's thought we must deal with him on his own. He was on his own early, from his teaching days forward. Notwithstanding our task here, and in spite of the difficulty of these two works, those who might be excited enough by discussions such as this one to make their own study of Bonhoeffer's writings will find themselves well advised to include these works in their labors.

1. Analogia Relationis

In all, the time during which Bonhoeffer's central concern was his teaching at the University of Berlin saw him give nine courses, four seminars and five series of lectures. Of the latter, the third was entitled "Creation and Sin: Theological Interpretation of Genesis 1–3." (The title "Creation and Fall" was adopted later for publication purposes.) Pivotal for this discussion was Bonhoeffer's concept of the *analogia relationis*, the "analogy of relationship." We must now examine the argument that brought it to the fore.

For Bonhoeffer there is only one option open to Christians in approaching the opening chapters of Genesis, and that is the vantage point of the Church and its faith in Christ. The subject matter is creation, and creation speaks of the beginning. But Christians can wrestle with the question of the beginning only with Christ in mind. "The church sees creation from Christ out," [4] as he puts it. That is to say, "in the fallen, old world it believes in the new creation world of the beginning and of the end, because it believes in Christ and in nothing else" (CF 11–12).

Such is the burden of the brief introduction to the lectures. The treatment of Genesis 1–3 has as its concern the explication of what faith in Christ has to do with the understanding of creation. Or, to state the same thing more technically, it has to do with a christological understanding of creation. This is what Bonhoeffer was pointing to in the subtitle of the work. He is attempting a *theological* interpretation of these chapters. His broad point is a striking one: There is only one link between God and the world, and that is God's freedom. *This* freedom is known in Christ.

What at first glance may appear to be an impossible limitation, excluding all but a narrowly defined Christian viewpoint for coming to terms with the opening lines of the *Old* Testament, is in fact a liberation. Bonhoeffer's goal is to bring to bear the freedom of God on the explication of creation. With this in mind he is able to begin with what any perceptive interpretation of Genesis 1 must include, namely, the irritation these lines must hold for man. For these lines speak to man of something he neither can nor does know. They speak to him of a beginning, and he is not in the beginning, he is *in the middle*, between a lost beginning and a doubtful end: "Man no longer lives in the beginning—he has lost the beginning. Now he finds he is in the middle, knowing neither the end nor the beginning, and yet knowing that he is in the middle, coming from the beginning and going towards the end. He sees that his life is determined by these two facets, of which he knows only that he does not know them" (CF 14).

All conversation both about God and about creation must take place "in the middle" where man is. Otherwise both "God" and "creation" will be abstractions. In insisting on this Bonhoeffer sounds one of the great themes that is a constant in all that he says, including, as we shall see, even the shattering questions of his prison writings: God is present, not remote. "In the beginning—God. That is true if he is present to us in the middle with this word as the one who creates and not as one who is remote, reposing, eternally being. We can only *know* of the beginning in the true sense as we hear of it in the middle between beginning and end" (CF 16). This is why the emphasis must fall on the *freedom* of God. The problem of creation, accordingly, is neither chronological nor causal in character. It is, rather, the problem of the freedom of God's act.

This quite unrepeatable, unique, free event in the beginning, which must not be confused in any way with the year 4004 or any similar particular date, is the creation. *In the beginning God created the heavens and the earth.* That means that the Creator, in freedom, creates the creature. Their connexion is not conditioned by anything except freedom, which means that it is unconditioned. Hence every use of a causal category for understanding the act of creation is ruled out (CF 17–18).

If chronological and causal reflections offer no clue to creation, what does? Only that which discloses the freedom of God. This is the heart of Bonhoeffer's christological understanding of creation. The resurrection of Jesus Christ is the focus of God's freedom "in the middle." It is accordingly the clue to God's freedom in the act of creation. In this sense Bonhoeffer could and did insist that the creation stands under the sign of the resurrection. His formulation contains one of his most penetrating insights:

> From the beginning the world is placed in the sign of the resurrection of Christ from the dead. Indeed it is because we know of the resurrection that we know of God's creation in the beginning, of God's creation out of nothing. The dead Jesus Christ of Good Friday—and the resurrected *kurios* (Lord) of Easter Sunday: that is creation out of nothing, creation from the beginning. . . . There is absolutely no transition or continuity between the dead and the resurrected Christ except the freedom of God which, in the beginning, created his work out of nothing (CF 19).

Against this background Bonhoeffer unfolded his concept of the *analogia relationis*. Theology will always be faced with the problem of analogy. Indeed, one could say that this is its inexhaustible problem. How does one speak of God in human language? Where are the similarities between man's existence and God's being, seeing that man is who and what he is? The classical theological tradition has always wrestled with this, and one of its perplexities was and is to come to terms with the unforgettable language of the opening chapter of Genesis and its astonishing suggestion that man is created in the image of God. Genesis 1:26–27, the passage suggesting this celebrated phrase, received a memorable treatment from Bonhoeffer's hand. With Christology as the clue to the doctrine of creation, the focus is on freedom. One could put it this way, then: In creation minus man God could behold his work but not a reflection of himself. "Only in something that is itself free can the One who is free, the Creator, see himself" (CF 36). If this freedom is a reflection of the Creator's freedom, then the freedoms must correspond. If Christ is the clue to the nature of God's freedom, he is also the clue to the nature of man's freedom. And this is of immense import. For God in Christ is understandable only in his relationship to man. So man in Christ is also understandable only in his relationship to God. "God in Christ is free for man. Because he does not retain his freedom for himself the concept of freedom only exists for us as 'being free for'. For us who live in the middle through Christ and know our humanity in his resurrection, that God is free has no meaning except that we are free for God" (CF 37–38).

How then is this a matter of *analogy?* For Bonhoeffer, the relationship between God and man is itself understandable only in terms of the relationship between man and man. This relational character of man has been woven into his very creaturehood. "Man is free by the fact that creature is related to creature. Man is free for man, *Male and female he created them.* Man is not alone, he is in duality and it is in this dependence on the other that his creatureliness consists" (CF 38). Thus, the concept of man in the image of God cannot be discerned by analyzing man the individual. Man cannot be himself by himself! Accordingly, the human reflection of God is not to be found in man the individual but only in man in relation to his fellow man. And it is this *relationship* that reflects God's relationship with man. Here alone is the point of analogy.

In setting out his understanding of this, Bonhoeffer emphasized his argument by explicitly rejecting the classical tradition's most hoary notion on the matter. This is the *analogia entis*, the "analogy of being," which attempts to find correspondences in man's individuality with the being of God.

[51]

Bonhoeffer's point is ruthlessly clear. There is no parallel between man's being in-and-for-himself and the being of God. That is to say, there is no way via analogy from man the individual to God the Creator. In commenting on the pivotal phrase in Genesis 1:27, then, he rejected the analogy of being (*analogia entis*) and in its place spoke of the analogy of relationship (*analogia relationis*). "The 'image . . . after our likeness' is consequently not an *analogia entis* in which man, in his being *per se* and *a se* [*An-und-für-sich-sein*], is in the likeness of the being of God. There is no such analogy between God and man. . . . The likeness, the analogy of man to God, is not *analogia entis* but *analogia relationis*" (CF 38).[5] As the relational character of man's creaturehood is the free gift of the God who in freedom creates, so is the analogy of relationship. It derives from and is dependent upon God's act. In the light of the knowledge of this act, however—in the light, that is, of God as he is known in Christ—it can be said that man in his freedom for the other is man in the image of God.

All analogies have a reversible character. That is their danger. Bonhoeffer would be the last to suggest that the relationship between man and fellow man can independently illuminate the relationship between God and man in Christ. Nor may we. Nevertheless it must be noted that the concept now before us tells us much about the state of Bonhoeffer's theological reflections when, as he turned twenty-six in the winter of 1931–1932, he put together the lectures containing this striking idea. To be sure, Christology can and does unfold only in the reflection on an act initiated, so to say, from God's side. Even so, for Bonhoeffer there never was or will be a time when what happens in Jesus Christ can be understood apart from the world of man. In suggesting that the *relation* between God and man is *the* clue to man's uniqueness as the creature God makes in his own image, Bonhoeffer is at the same time insisting on a *relational understanding* of Christology itself. Now as we shall see in the next chapter, the fact is that this is true of his Christology from the earliest of his writings on through the theological work he did in the midst of his participation in the conspiracy against the Third Reich. The extent to which he will press the point is already before us here. For Bonhoeffer, *concreteness* is the abiding mark of the center of the faith and all that it implies. For relationships may be discussed ethically. Indeed, is there any other way to discuss them? Accordingly, Bonhoeffer's Christology has a markedly ethical coloration. So does all theology, for that matter, if his point regarding the analogy of relationship holds.

We have here noted two things that must be emphasized. In the first place, the concept of the analogy of relationship entails the radical resistance against all abstraction in theology. This is what has always been wrong with the traditional concept of the analogy of being. Man in and for himself is an abstraction. The only real man is the concrete man who springs out of the relationships that constitute him. So, at least, Bonhoeffer seems to be saying, and all who see his point can hardly resist the implication. The God who in freedom creates *this* man in his image is himself understandable only in relational terms.

In the second place, and here we must be extremely careful in the way we put it, the kind of theological reflection that can yield an idea like the analogy of relationship is more than simply ethical in tone, it is ethical in content from start to finish. Bonhoeffer is a key figure in what could be called the ethicizing of theology. This is not to be confused with the *replacement* of theology by ethics. That would be a distortion, and would in fact represent the extreme of a fallacious reversal of the analogy. What is rather at stake is the *ethical intensification* of all theological concepts. There are others before and after Bonhoeffer who have labored in their own ways on this front—Emil Brunner, Reinhold Niebuhr, Karl Barth (who would later make much use of Bonhoeffer's analogy of relationship, in III/1 and III/2 of the *Church Dogmatics*, though he would put a twist on it that Bonhoeffer would not have countenanced), and Paul Lehmann, and the list could be expanded to include both earlier and more recent figures. But however one treats this broad line of effort, certainly Bonhoeffer is decisive in the emergence of its cogency. This is already patent in the concept before us. It becomes even more so in his understanding of the connection between faith and obedience, in *The Cost of Discipleship*, to which we now turn.

2. Faith and Obedience

The Finkenwalde days brought forth two major works from Bonhoeffer's hand—*Life Together* (*Gemeinsames Leben*), on which we shall comment later, and *The Cost of Discipleship* (*Nachfolge*). The latter, as we have indicated, is the book by which Bonhoeffer was best known during his lifetime. Bethge notes that these two books taken together are the decisive yield of the second phase of Bonhoeffer's life, the transition from theologian to Christian, as we have seen him formulate it.[6] Bonhoeffer's major concern in *The Cost of Discipleship* is with the Sermon on the Mount, which he discusses at length in the second section of the book. This is introduced by a section on "Grace and Discipleship," and it is followed by a treatment of Matthew 9:35–10:42 entitled "The Messengers," and a concluding section on "The Church of Jesus Christ and the Life of Discipleship."[7] Our concern is with the initial section, on "Grace and Discipleship," which contains one of the most lucid and bold explications of the relationship between faith and obedience ever written.

It is important to know in approaching this book that later, from his prison cell, Bonhoeffer would have second thoughts about it. As we have seen in setting out the sketch of his life, Bonhoeffer and the others in the conspiracy knew the shattering disappearance of hope with the failure of the attempt on Hitler's life on July 20, 1944. Bethge lifts up the letter of the following day, July 21, as crucial for understanding the ultimate reaches of the man and his faith and thought. One can only agree. The key passage of this letter for our present considerations runs as follows:

[54]

I remember a conversation that I had in America thirteen years ago with a young French pastor. We were asking ourselves quite simply what we wanted to do with our lives. He said he would like to become a saint (and I think it is quite likely that he did become one). At that time I was very impressed but I disagreed with him, and said, in effect, that I should like to learn to have faith. For a long time I did not realize the depth of the contrast. I thought I could acquire faith by trying to live a holy life, or something like it. I suppose I wrote *The Cost of Discipleship* as the end of that path. Today I can see the dangers of that book, though I still stand by what I wrote (LP 193).[8]

Obviously, any attempt to deal with *The Cost of Discipleship* must reckon with this remark. This is particularly the case for a discussion such as ours which seeks to discern the *promise* of Bonhoeffer's theology. The real issue can be put simply: What is the *permanent* yield of this book? Our argument should likewise be stated simply: The permanent yield is the understanding Bonhoeffer reached regarding the relationship between faith and obedience. The fact is, as we shall see, that Bonhoeffer isolated in this work what proved to be the dynamic, the animating principle, of his life *and* his theology. It had already been in operation. It would continue to the end. And knowledge of it entails the decisive clue to the puzzling and exciting suggestions he reached, both in the sketches for the proposed *Ethics* and in his prison writings. Conversely, failure to recognize the significance of the point at hand will lead to the misunderstanding of the celebrated flashes of insight from the closing years of his life.

The Cost of Discipleship commences with what has become a classic distinction, the distinction between *cheap* and *costly* grace. This is no doubt the reason for the title of the English translation. *Nachfolge* means simply "discipleship," and one could wish that the title had been rendered this way, since this is what Bonhoeffer called the book. However that may be, the title of the translation aptly focuses the point of departure of the discussion. All too long much of Protestantism in general,

and certainly classical Lutheranism in particular, has absolut-
ized Luther's profound insight into the argument of Paul's
Letter to the Romans and its abiding basis, *justification by
faith alone* (or more properly, justification by grace through
faith). That man is redeemed by God's free act and that his
life must be the response to this is the hallmark of the
Reformation. The trouble is that one can forget the second
half of this way of putting it, and if one does, the inexorable
result is that in the light of the grace of God in Jesus Christ
one does—nothing.

This phenomenon has a storied past, and with its consequences Bonhoeffer had lost patience. Grace alone—yes! But
only in terms of the life that this grace must yield. For without
the latter, grace has been cheapened, one forgets its *cost*. The
Bonhoeffer who had been to London and back in his own
involvement in the Church Struggle, and who was then
charged with the perilous operation at Finkenwalde—and the
Bonhoeffer who knew his own tradition inside out, and could
handle it already with the skill of a theological virtuoso—this
Bonhoeffer now mobilized his creativity for a book on *discipleship*. The lines containing the distinction between *cheap
grace* and *costly grace* are memorable, and should not be ex-
cised. The reader who has come this far in this discussion
probably already knows them. If not, he should cease reading
this and go find them (cf. CD 45–48). Here only the heart of
the point may be cited: the delineation of the grace of which
the New Testament speaks, grace that is real, grace that is
costly:

> Costly grace is the gospel which must be *sought* again and again,
> the gift which must be *asked* for, the door at which a man must
> *knock*.

> Such grace is *costly* because it calls us to follow, and it is *grace*
> because it calls us to follow *Jesus Christ*. It is costly because it
> cost a man his life, and it is grace because it gives a man the only
> true life. It is costly because it condemns sin, and grace because
> it justifies the sinner. Above all, it is *costly* because it cost God

[56]

the life of his Son: "ye were bought at a price", and what has cost God much cannot be cheap for us. Above all, it is *grace* because God did not reckon his Son too dear a price to pay for our life, but delivered him up for us. Costly grace is the Incarnation of God (CD 47–48).[9]

The Cost of Discipleship, especially the long treatment of the Sermon on the Mount, sets out what Bonhoeffer saw all this to entail as Finkenwalde raced toward its demise. The crucial point for us is the initial insight to which he moved, given the insistence on the basic issue, that grace is costly. This is his understanding of the *call* to discipleship. In a word, the summons *and* the response to it *precede* faith. Indeed, the summons and the response to it together form the precondition of faith. The disciples found out who Jesus was only by following him. In Bonhoeffer's matchless sentence, "The disciple simply burns his boats and goes ahead" (CD 62). This puts him "in the situation where faith is possible" (CD 67). Everything depends in the first instance on the call itself, for discipleship in its only real sense is the gift of the one who calls. Reflecting on this caused Bonhoeffer to struggle for real precision, for it is "extremely hazardous" to discern where faith is possible, and where it is not (CD 68). This led him to the decisive formulation: "The idea of a situation in which faith is possible is only a way of stating the facts of a case in which the following two propositions hold good and are equally true: *only he who believes is obedient, and only he who is obedient believes*" (CD 69).

Bonhoeffer's elaboration of this formulation is of the utmost significance, both for understanding the subsequent development of his thought and for grasping his contribution to theology at large. The passage is lengthy and we must cite it in its entirety. As we do so, two observations should be noted carefully. First, Bonhoeffer means the formulation exactly as stated, without any equivocation. *Both* propositions are true, and each is valid only while and to the extent that the other is. Second, the thrust of Bonhoeffer's insight lies in his perception that belief or faith and obedience may be *logically* but

not *chronologically* separated. The elaboration follows immediately after the formulation just noted, and it reads this way:

> It is quite unbiblical to hold the first proposition without the
> second. We think we understand when we hear that obedience
> is possible only where there is faith. Does not obedience follow
> faith as good fruit grows on a good tree? First, faith, then obedi-
> ence. If by that we mean that it is faith which justifies, and not
> the act of obedience, all well and good, for that is the essential
> and unexceptionable presupposition of all that follows. If, how-
> ever, we make a chronological distinction between faith and
> obedience, and make obedience subsequent to faith, we are
> divorcing the one from the other—and then we get the practical
> question, when must obedience begin? Obedience remains sepa-
> rated from faith. From the point of view of justification it is
> necessary thus to separate them, but we must never lose sight of
> their essential unity. For faith is only real when there is obedi-
> ence, never without it, and faith only becomes faith in the act of
> obedience (CD 69).

For Bonhoeffer, then, faith exists only as obedience. (This
is, in fact, the way he puts it—". . . Glaude nur im
Gehorsam existiert . . ." [10]—rather than "faith is only real
when there is obedience" as in the translation.) By way of
emphasizing the issue at hand, Bonhoeffer made a striking
addition when he reached this point in his elaboration. What
we have before us is enough to underscore the dialectical
relation between the two propositions. That is, it is enough
to mark his insistence that these are dependent upon each
other so that neither is correct by itself. There is a hidden
depth, however, in the contention that faith does not hold
chronological priority over obedience. This is already intimated
in the assertion that the practical question, *When* must obedience begin? is the wrong question. If neither holds chronological priority over the other then either may come first!
That is to say, the relationship between faith and obedience
is absolutely reversible. Bonhoeffer put it thus:

> Since, then, we cannot adequately speak of obedience as the
> consequence of faith, and since we must never forget the indis-

soluble unity of the two, we must place the one proposition that only he who believes is obedient alongside the other, that only he who is obedient believes. In the one case faith is the condition of obedience, and in the other obedience the condition of faith. In exactly the same way in which obedience is called the consequence of faith, it must also be called the presupposition of faith (CD 69–70).

Had he never written another line this would be enough to assure Bonhoeffer's place as a creative theologian of major significance. But he did write more, because he lived beyond the context of his thought in 1937. Faith and obedience go hand in hand, each is alive, each feeds the other. As Bonhoeffer's sphere of obedience extended, so did his faith. As his faith deepened, so did his obedience. The analogy of relationship could not be reversed, but the relationship between faith and obedience had to be, for it is fluid, it is alive. Belief informs context even as context informs belief. This is the precise reason why the story of Bonhoeffer's life is intrinsic to the discussion of his theology. One cannot grasp his understanding of the Christian faith without beholding the obedience that accompanied it. Of course, then, he would come to a time when he questioned some of the theology of *The Cost of Discipleship*, and thus recognized the "dangers" of the book—he had lived, believed, obeyed beyond it.

Analogia relationis, Faith and Obedience—these are key ideas from the time before Bonhoeffer's involvement in the conspiracy. Clearly, it would be an absurdity to suggest that the period up to 1938 was one of stability, except by comparison with the chaos and torment that followed. Whereas these are not "early" insights in the sense that they spring from Bonhoeffer's very first attempts at theological construction, they nevertheless represent conclusions reached before the radical unfolding of the context that would stretch his creativity to its greatest extent. It is important, then, to emphasize that they were worked out before the days of the conspiracy and the crucible of the Tegel cell. This "modern" theologian had already put to work his training at the hands of liberal theology. Both ideas are *relational,* and thus drive toward an understanding of the Christian faith that is profoundly social in character. But this is not their only component. Both ideas are profoundly christological as well. This theologian who knew his debt to the liberals was also "modern," responsive, that is, to a new mood. It has been impossible to get at either of these arguments without laying hold of the fact that they are attempts to make sense out of belief in Jesus Christ.

It is to this christological dimension of Bonhoeffer's thought that we now turn more directly. In so doing we must bring into our purview the writings of his closing years. For the question is, What happened to the thinking that could yield concepts such as these as it moved inexorably down the road toward the gallows? Or, to utilize Bethge's unforgettable insight, What happened to the theology of a theologian who became a contemporary? The question cannot be answered without coming to terms with Bonhoeffer's understanding of the uniqueness and significance of the Christ.

III.

The Reality of Christ

This chapter title has two meanings. There is the reality of Christ himself, and there is the reality of the world in the light of him. Both are always present in Bonhoeffer's thought. His Christology was always worldly, and his respect for and understanding of the world was always informed by the transcending dimension of his faith in Christ.

We can now see that for this theologian all theology, especially all Christology, will be dynamic, fluid, and open-ended. The remark must be handled with care, for this is true of any theology worth its salt. The subject matter of theology is alive, and therefore defies any final formulation. The theologian's task is to deal with this dynamic subject matter as coherently and consistently as possible. But no *final* system is ever possible. In the case of Bonhoeffer, sensitivity to this is built into everything that he writes.

At the same time it is extremely necessary to be clear on what we are not saying. In the face of the fragmentary character of the writings from the time of the conspiracy and prison it must be remembered that Bonhoeffer was a systematic theologian in the most rigorous sense of the term. His posthumously published writings are fragmentary because he wrote them in the midst of chaos—*Ethics* just before and during the time of the trips for the conspiracy, and the *Letters and Papers* from the cell at Tegel. Necessity dictated the fragmentary form, not some hostility on Bonhoeffer's part toward the basic task of stating his theology with coherence and consistency. There can be no doubt of this, given his training and earlier work. Moreover, radical though it was, his Christology was grounded in a profound grasp of the traditional attempts to state the uniqueness and significance of Jesus Christ. Had he survived the fall of the Third Reich he would have written out his work *systematically*. It is forceful and unforgettable enough as it stands. Had he been able to state it comprehensively it would have been even more so.

The subject of Bonhoeffer's Christology is broad and complex. Here our goal of discerning the *promise* of his thought must dictate our procedure. We shall look first at the understanding he reached by the time he worked on the *Ethics*, and this will be before us in the first two sections of our discussion. In the third section we shall indicate the roots of this understanding in his earlier works. This will prepare the way for Chapters IV and V, in which we shall be confronted with the far reaches of his thought. This procedure suggests the basic fact informing this, and any, treatment of the issue at hand. Christology is the unifying element running throughout the whole of Bonhoeffer's work.

1. Christ and Reality

Our first task is to see that by the time of the work on the *Ethics* Bonhoeffer had reached an unshakable conclusion: Christ and reality go together. This is not to say that Christ does not transcend the world. It is with Christ and reality, in that order, that we must begin if we are to be true to his thought. Even so, one notes that at every turn this transcendence is not self-contained. Bonhoeffer simply cannot talk about the transcending Christ, even when he is using the most widely received biblical and traditional phraseology, without talking about the world at the same time. Indeed the central and basic issue is simply the fact that Christ is the point at which God and the world must be discussed together. The *Ethics* abounds with statements to this effect. One of the most important is as follows:

No man can look with undivided vision at God and at the world of reality so long as God and the world are torn asunder.

Try as he may, he can only let his eyes wander distractedly from one to the other. But there is a place at which God and the cosmic reality are reconciled, a place at which God and man have become one. That and that alone is what enables man to set his eyes upon God and the world at the same time. This place does not lie somewhere out beyond reality in the realm of ideas. It lies in the midst of history as a divine miracle. It lies in Jesus Christ, the Reconciler of the world. . . . Whoever sees Jesus Christ does indeed see God and the world in one. He can henceforward no longer see God without the world or the world without God (E 69–70).

Everything depends on what is meant by the word "world," and this is *the* crucial thing to say about this formulation. We can only get at Bonhoeffer's Christology while getting at "reality"! Unlike much that has gone before and come since, Bonhoeffer's efforts at Christology juxtapose Christ and reality so closely that the explication of the latter is part of the explication of the former. To be sure, *reality* here is not self-evident. Something new and unexpected is in its midst, something transforming, something liberating, and that is Christ. But the identity, the uniqueness, the significance of Christ know no possibility of formulation apart from the reality that is being changed. Bonhoeffer does not state his Christology and then plug it into the world. That would be to leave God and the world "torn asunder." He attempts, rather, to state Christology and the changing reality simultaneously.

The discussion leading into the passage just noted is a good demonstration of this, but we will save it for analysis at the beginning of the next section. For there is a better example that demands attention here. Everything depends on the word "world," we have said. That is true, but it has a precise meaning. Everything depends on the world as it appears when one beholds it in Christ, where God and the world must be seen together. Reality in general and reality in Christ are not the same. The contrast is drastic. However it is *not* abstract. In the light of what we have seen so far there should be little mystery to the fact that Bonhoeffer stated this contrast in ethical terms. Of the many indications of this in the *Ethics* one of the very best for our consideration at this point is the penetrating insight he developed into the contrast between Jesus and the Pharisees.

Bonhoeffer led into this discussion by reiterating the point in the citation we have just noted. This reiteration is the culmination of his argument that conflict—specifically the conflict between good and evil—is *not* the basis of ethical decision in the New Testament (E 17ff.). "Not man's falling apart from God, from men, from things and from himself, but rather the rediscovered unity, reconciliation, is now the basis of the discussion and the 'point' of decision of the specifically ethical experience" (E 26). His meaning is clarified in the discussion of "Jesus's encounter with the Pharisees," to which he immediately proceeds, noting as he does so that "The correct understanding of this encounter is of the greatest significance for the understanding of the gospel as a whole" (E 26).[1] Bonhoeffer characterized the Pharisee as "that extremely admirable man who subordinates his entire life to his knowledge of good and evil and is as severe a judge of himself as of his neighbour to the honour of God, whom he humbly thanks for this knowledge" (E 27). The Pharisee's problem, to which he devotes the entire momentum of his life, is the problem of this conflict and the decision necessary to overcome it. This explains the continuous and unresolvable argument between him and Jesus. He is preoccupied, anxiously so, with an issue Jesus has left behind, and Jesus is speaking in terms of a reality he either cannot or will not recognize.

> The crucial point about all these arguments is that Jesus does not allow Himself to be drawn into a single one of these conflicts and decisions. With each of His answers He simply leaves the case of conflict beneath Him. . . . Just as the Pharisees cannot do otherwise than confront Jesus with situations of conflict, so, too, Jesus cannot do otherwise than refuse to accept these situations. Just as the Pharisees' question and temptation arises from the disunion of the knowledge of good and evil, so, too, Jesus's answer arises from unity with God, with the origin, and from the

[64]

overcoming of the disunion of man with God. The Pharisees and Jesus are speaking on totally different levels (E 28).

The confrontation is radical. Once seen it leaves one forever faced with the tangibly transcendent claim on which the Christian faith is based. To be sure, conflict remains, but it has itself been transmuted. It is now the conflict between differing realities, the one for which God and man are reunited, the other for which God and man are still separated. For the latter the problem is for man to reach God by way of the integrity and constancy of his own decisions, for the former the challenge is for man to decide in the light of the fact that God has reached him. It is this new reality that Jesus embodies and seeks to express. This is why he refuses to be trapped inside the problem of the wrong reality. The words of the antagonists "fail to make contact." Indeed, "Jesus's answers do not appear to be answers at all, but rather attacks of His own against the Pharisees, which is what they, in fact, are" (E 28). This is the root of one of the most basic, pronounced, and unavoidable elements of the gospel: ". . . in the New Testament there is no single question put by men to Jesus which Jesus answers with an acceptance of the human either-or that every such question implies" (E 29).

Christ transcends the world; he brings to it what it cannot yield for itself. He reunites man with God. Such is the claim of the Christian faith. To talk about the confrontation between Jesus and the Pharisees puts flesh and blood on this claim. The new reality is not out there somewhere; it is in the midst of the human struggle with the ethical question. To speak about "the overcoming of the disunion of man with God" will be a meaningless, pious abstraction unless one sees that this entails abrasive conflict with those obsessed with the question of good and evil. When one does see this abrasive confrontation, then the phrase becomes a pointer, an attempt to indicate the astonishing possibility that looms up beyond the good-and-evil barrier.

Something of the genius of Bonhoeffer's Christology as it took shape in the sketches for the *Ethics* is before us here. In his efforts to state the uniqueness and significance of Jesus Christ there is both need and room for the discussion of the world, so much so that the latter discussion is intrinsic to the former. The reality that Christ is, is as alive as the reality he discloses. Hence the reality that Christ is, is always capable of further development, further extension. This is hardly pressing the point too far. One could expect it to be this way for a theologian who had already challenged the chronological priority of faith over obedience. But we must examine this more closely lest we misunderstand Bonhoeffer's insight at its deepest levels.

2. Reality in Christ

There is perhaps more than meets the eye to our reversal of the theme. Reality *in* Christ is what we must ponder now. Just as Christ cannot be discussed apart from the consequences of his coming, so the world as it *really* is cannot be discussed apart from Christ. This too is part of the drastic claim made by the Christian faith. But this means that something is afoot in the concept of reality—something that blends what man *knows* with the transformation of what man knows in the light of Christ. What is the reality that is the consequence of the reality that is Christ? If Christ is not to be the prisoner of the reality that is immediately apparent, what then is the reality that he discloses and without which he cannot be understood?

Our second task in coming to terms with Bonhoeffer's Christology is to deal with this question. For there is more to his Christology than simply a new and perceptive interpretation of the Bible and of the classical theological language of the church. He moved beyond the frontiers marked on the received maps and explored terrain beyond the known limits. The factor that accounts for this, more than any other, was his insatiable curiosity about the world as it appears in the light of Christ.

An important clue to what is involved here is to be found in connection with the first passage cited in the preceding section. "No man can look with undivided vision at God and at the world of reality so long as God and the world are torn asunder" (E 69). When he wrote this, Bonhoeffer already had some clear ideas as to what unfolds before one's eyes when God and the world are *not* torn asunder but viewed together. This is explicity indicated in the reflection on simplicity and wisdom that immediately precedes these words. "To be simple is to fix one's eyes solely on the simple truth of God at a time when all concepts are being confused, distorted and turned upside down" (E 68). Such simplicity, though, is free to behold what is going on with penetrating perception, which, argued Bonhoeffer, is how it becomes wisdom. The important point for us to note is how he understands wisdom. "It is precisely because [the simple man] looks only to God, without any sidelong glance at the world, that he is able to look at the reality of the world freely and without prejudice. And that is how simplicity becomes wisdom. The wise man is the one who sees reality as it is, and who sees into the depths of things. That is why only that man is wise who sees reality in God" (E 68).

These words will sound tame, pious, even platitudinous, if one forgets that they are written by a theologian explicitly committed to perilous trips across the German border for the conspiracy against Hitler's demonic state. Simple wisdom indeed! For Bonhoeffer "the depths of things" is hardly a mere metaphor. Nor is the formulation that follows. The reality he is speaking of has to do with "the essential nature of things," and this phrase is not shackled to a static, metaphysical notion of the ultimate. It, rather, turns on the recognition of "the significant" in the midst of "the factual": "To understand reality is not the same as to know about outward events. It is to perceive the essential nature of things. . . . And so the wise man will seek to acquire the best possible knowledge about events, but always without becoming dependent upon this knowledge. To recognize the significant in the factual is wisdom" (E 68–69).

To discern the significant in the midst of the factual is a christological question as far as Bonhoeffer is concerned. This could well be construed as the central thrust both of his Christology and of his ethics. The factual must be given its due, but without the Christ it will fall short of the ultimate reality, the reality of God.

Here we must at last face critically the fascinating issue of Bonhoeffer's thought. It has been with us all along, but we are now at the point where it can and must be stated explicitly. As Bonhoeffer's life and work developed he was both continually and increasingly preoccupied with the *ethical* side of the broad Christian claim, to the extent that in the closing years of his life everything that he wrote had to do with the clarification of the ethical frontier of Christian conviction. Some will regard this as a limitation, even a reduction of sorts. Some will regard it as an accident that manifests only the uncompleted state of his work, and indicates that had he lived there would have been more to say on other facets of Christian truth. And some will regard it as his most lasting contribution. The present writer regards the first of these as totally wrong, and the second incapable of demonstration. (The only assumption that can be risked about what Bonhoeffer might have done had he lived on is that he would have worked systematically, in the sense noted at the outset of this chapter.) The point of view of this discussion, then, is that Bonhoeffer's preoccupation with the ethical frontier of Christian theology does not represent a reduction of theology but an expansion of ethics. The concept of reality is decisive for this case. It would have been impossible for Bonhoeffer to make his point in a traditionally metaphysical fashion, for the words would have been hollow and abstract. To be sure, it was difficult enough for him to say what he meant in his own way, that is, ethically. But one thing is clear. The words are not hollow.

Bonhoeffer attacked the point frontally in one of the truly

pivotal sections of the *Ethics*. This section, entitled "Christ, Reality and Good" (with the subtitle, "Christ, the Church and the World") contains some of the most important material in the work. Here we are concerned with the initial subsection on "The Concept of Reality." (We will return to the other two subsections in the next chapter.) Bonhoeffer's point of departure is with what we may call the transformation of the ethical question. The ethical question is no longer "How can I be good?" or "How can I do good?" It is, rather, "What is the will of God?" Nothing is quite so irritating as this, the standard initial maneuver of all Christian ethicists, for precisely the reason that Bonhoeffer cites. What the new question presupposes is "a decision with regard to ultimate reality . . . a decision of faith" (E 186). Nothing is quite so irritating, that is, unless he means the equation he suggests, namely, that the decision of faith and the decision about ultimate reality are one and the same. And he means it.

> . . . the problem of ethics at once assumes a new aspect if it becomes apparent that these realities, myself and the world, themselves lie embedded in a quite different reality, namely, the reality of God, the Creator, Reconciler and Redeemer. What is of ultimate importance is now no longer that I should become good, or that the condition of the world should be made better by my action, but that the reality of God should show itself everywhere to be the ultimate reality (E 188).

The force of this assertion must not be overlooked. If Bonhoeffer is correct then the *reality of God* can be shown—by man. This is the point of Christian ethics. It is also the point of our remark that Bonhoeffer's words are not hollow. What is at stake is a demonstrable ultimate reality. Participation in this ultimate reality is *the* gift of God in Christ to man. This insight is the very heart of Bonhoeffer's Christology.

> In Christ we are offered the possibility of partaking in the reality of God and in the reality of the world, but not in the one without the other. The reality of God discloses itself only by setting me entirely in the reality of the world, and when I encounter

the reality of the world it is always already sustained, accepted and reconciled in the reality of God. This is the inner meaning of the revelation of God in the man Jesus Christ (E 195).

The "inner meaning" of the revelation—better, the "secret" of the revelation, since this is Bonhoeffer's word (*Geheimnis*[2]). In either case, though, the point is clear. What is offered to man in Christ is the presence of the ultimate reality, in which he has a part to play.

But what does that mean? The whole of the *Ethics*, and for that matter, of the *Letters and Papers from Prison* as well, is Bonhoeffer's attempt to answer this. Presently, in Chapters IV and V, we shall set out in some detail how this runs. For the moment, though, two decisive points lie close at hand, and they should be noted in this immediate context.

(1) Bonhoeffer was clear on what it did *not* mean. Earlier we heard him say that wisdom has to do with the recognition of the significant in the factual. Now without doubt, for Bonhoeffer it is the Christ who is in the midst of the factual that is *the* clue to this significance. But this makes sense only if the factual itself is taken with the utmost seriousness. Bonhoeffer was willing to make common cause with those whose sole concern is with things as they are in one very basic sense. "It is reality that teaches what is good" (E 194). This puts him squarely in the camp of the positivists and empiricists, as over against the idealists, for they are always "closer to reality" than is any idealistic attempt to realize the unreal. However, in saying this, Bonhoeffer was careful to state the limits of the factual by itself. "It now transpires that the concept of reality which underlies the positivistic ethics is the meretricious concept of the empirically verifiable, which implies denial of the origin of this reality in the ultimate reality, in God" (E 194).

As every student of language knows, all translations are commentaries. Here the translator has actually intensified Bonhoeffer's assertion, perhaps to the point of distortion. He renders Bonhoeffer's phrase, *der vulgäre Begriff*[3] as "the meretricious concept." The word *vulgär* means the same thing in

German that it does in English: "vulgar." *Meretricious,* on the other hand, is derived from the Latin *meretrix,* meaning "prostitute." "Vulgar" can have this meaning, but this narrows Bonhoeffer's point. What the translation makes him say is that the world of the factual, that which is empirically verifiable, is at best only apparently attractive, deceitfully alluring. This is implied by Bonhoeffer's own choice of words, but the matter should be left the way he put it himself. The factual alone is common, prosaic, even base. Any ethic that is concerned *only* with the facts as they are will tend to operate with only expediency in mind.

Ultimate reality is more demanding. Reality in Christ has to do with what is in the midst of what is! This reality must be visible. It must be there for anyone to see, especially if he looks with all the precision of thoroughgoing empirical analysis. Otherwise this reality is not *real.* Specifically, though, where and how is *this* reality to be seen in fact? Where, that is, does the reality of God in Christ enter the world in such a way that those who are preoccupied with facts alone can see it?

(2) Even to state the question as we just have is to intimate the only answer Bonhoeffer would countenance. No treatment of his Christology is complete that does not come to terms with his understanding of the Church. His understanding of Christ and his understanding of the Church coincide.

The most incisive statement of this in the *Ethics* occurs in Bonhoeffer's elaboration of his concept of *formation.* This is the crucial indication of what participation in the reality of God in Christ meant for him as he carried on his theological labors in the midst of the conspiracy. He formulated his basic equation succinctly: "To be conformed with the Incarnate— that is to be a real man" (E 81). Likewise he stated succinctly the conviction undergirding this: "God loves the real man. God became a real man" (E 81). The equation and the conviction informing it yield Bonhoeffer's version of the point to the gospel:

Man becomes man because God became man. But man does not become God. It is not he, therefore, who was or is able to accomplish his own transformation, but it is God who changes his form into the form of man, so that man may become, not indeed God, but, in the eyes of God, man.

In Christ there was re-created the form of man before God (E 82–83).

We dare not move over this passage too quickly. Real man equals man before God. God became man so that man could be before him. Christian faith is rooted in this, for, once it is seen, it can never be forgotten. It lingers forever as the inexhaustible possibility of a humanism that knows no parallel. The God of whom Christians try to speak is always cast in this human form, in such a way that to speak of him at all is to speak of a new humanity—the humanity comprised of those who stand before the God who is present.

But this grand possibility is a possibility only. For to state the point of the gospel of Christ in this way is also to encounter the predicament in which this possibility is always caught, and this is the entree, for Bonhoeffer, of the understanding of the Church. For him this turns on an astonishing phrase, "the longing of the Incarnate." The One who became man yearns to take form in all men. "It is a mystery, for which there is no explanation, that only a part of mankind recognize the form of their Redeemer. The longing of the Incarnate to take form in all men is as yet still unsatisfied. He bore the form of man as a whole, and yet He can take form only in a small band. These are His Church" (E 83). This yields Bonhoeffer's interpretation of the great Pauline concept of the Body of Christ, which he utilized to combine his idea of formation with his concept of reality. "The New Testament states the case profoundly and clearly when it calls the Church the Body of Christ. The body is the form. . . . The Church, then, bears the form which is in truth the proper form of all humanity. The image in which she is formed is the image of man. . . . The Church is nothing but a section of humanity in which Christ has *really* taken form" (E 83, italics added).

What Church? We may well ask! The point is radical and

polemical. One should be warned here, and Bonhoeffer was not at all reluctant to state the issue as vigorously as he knew how. A negative implication and a positive one spring immediately to the fore. These can be put with no equivocation. If Bonhoeffer is correct, and he is, then the Church must not be religious, it must be ethical. The negative implication is stated forcefully: "In the first instance, therefore, she has essentially nothing whatever to do with the so-called religious functions of man, but with the whole man in his existence in the world with all its implications. What matters in the Church is not religion but the form of Christ, and its taking form amidst a band of men" (E 83–84).

The positive implication, for which this paves the way, is stated with equal forcefulness. If the Church is not "a religious community of worshippers of Christ," what is it? Bonhoeffer knew that his own answer, it "is Christ Himself, who had taken form among men" (E 83), can have only an ethically colored meaning if it is to be *real* at all. "The point of departure for Christian ethics is the body of Christ, the form of Christ in the form of the Church, and the formation of the Church in conformity with the form of Christ" (E 84). Such an ethic must be concrete, the complete opposite of abstraction: "This leads us away from any kind of abstract ethic and towards an ethic which is entirely concrete. What can and must be said is not what is good once and for all, but the way in which Christ takes form among us here and now" (E 85). Such an ethic, the antonym of "religion" in Bonhoeffer's view, describes the reality of Christ, into which man is summoned as participant.

In the *Ethics* as well as in the *Letters and Papers from Prison*—during both the days of the conspiracy and the days of imprisonment—Bonhoeffer labored to extend further the understanding of the uniqueness and significance of Jesus Christ we now have before us. He moved even beyond the limits we have seen him reach, and our task now is to chart this movement. Before doing so it is important to pause for a brief backward look, in order to suggest where this understanding had its origins, and thus to indicate how it may be said that Christology is the unifying element in Bonhoeffer's work as a whole.

3. Early Foundations

What we have before us comes from the time of Bonhoeffer's total involvement in the risks of his closing years. Of course this had a profound effect on the process of theological reflection through which he moved. However, it is of truly prime importance to know that the radical Christology we are dealing with is *not* simply the result of this involvement. What is true of Bonhoeffer is true of all theological creativity (indeed, it is true of all human creativity of any sort). His insights were the product of his ability plus the context in which he worked. The *roots* of his pivotal christological concepts in the *Ethics* and beyond were explicitly present long before he made the momentous decision that night in New York to return to Germany. He took an already burgeoning creativity into his direct involvement in the mortal struggle against the Third Reich, and its focus was clearly on Christology. We have already seen an indication of this in discussing his concept of the analogy of relationship and his understanding of the relationship between faith and obedience. But we dare not leave the matter there, for the early and basic groundwork is even more apparent than these striking ideas show, and we are now in a position to see this.

We are, of course, equipped with all the wisdom of hindsight in making these observations. It would be naïve and misleading to suggest that everyone who read Bonhoeffer's dissertation or listened to his youthful lectures at Berlin knew immediately that they were dealing with a figure who would leave a revolutionary mark on theology. Such hero worship is out of place. It does no justice to the agonizingly slow work that goes into writing such as we have been attempting to interpret. Moreover, our discussion probably suggests far more homogeneity in the development of Bonhoeffer's thought than is in fact the case. Here we can only refer the reader, then, to broad and comprehensive treatments which have the scope for the detailed discussion that is in order.[4]

Granted this, we can make the basic point by noting three sets of passages. The first two come from Bonhoeffer's earliest works. The third is found in his lectures on Christology, given at Berlin in the summer of 1933.

Surely fundamental to all of Bonhoeffer's writings is the striking phrase "Christ existing as community" or "Christ existing as the church." (The German behind these is the same in each instance: *Christus als Gemeinde existierend*.[5] The latter translation is possible, since, in Bonhoeffer's contexts, *Gemeinde* can mean either "community" or "church," providing that one reads "church" to mean "fellowship of persons and not the institution." [6] The phrase received wide usage in his dissertation, *The Communion of Saints* (*Sanctorum Communio*), and it played a pivotal role in his second book, *Act and Being* (*Akt und Sein*). For reasons that we have noted earlier we shall not divert the present discussion into a broad analysis of either of these works (see pp. 47–48, above). But it is crucial for our purposes to take the measure of this particular idea.

In the dissertation, Bonhoeffer's subject was the doctrine of the Church. He sought to clarify the theological character of this doctrine in the face of any attempt to reduce it to sociologically limited analyses. At the same time he sought to do justice to the cogency with which the latter make their very significant contribution. In this effort one of his targets was Ernst Troeltsch, *the* pioneer figure in the attempt to combine theological and sociological insights.[7] We can catch a glimpse of what Bonhoeffer's phrase meant to him by noting his use of it in this context:

> The unity of the Christian church is not based upon the oneness of human spirits, but upon the unity of the divine spirit, and the two are not identical. In our discussion of the sociological type of community we showed that its ultimate unity was its being

as a collective person. This knowledge must be applied to the Christian religious community, as well as to the concept of the church; in the first case the course of the presentation would be from below upwards, whereas with the concept of the church it runs from above downwards. The personal unity of the church is "Christ existing as the church." Paul could even say that Christ himself is the church. A man is in Christ if he is in the church (CS 138).

The phrase offered Bonhoeffer a way of taking the basic sociological point seriously (i.e., community as collective person) while at the same time asserting the *theological* character of the concept of the Church. With the mighty phrases of the *Ethics* ringing in our ears, it is obvious that this is the groundwork for the grand assertion that "The Church is nothing but a section of humanity in which Christ has really taken form" (E 83).

Similarly illuminating is the use to which Bonhoeffer put the phrase in *Act and Being*. Here it enabled him to state his understanding of revelation.

The Christian communion is God's final revelation: God as "Christ existing as community," ordained for the rest of time until the end of the world and the return of Christ. It is here that Christ has come the nearest to humanity, here given himself to his new humanity, so that his person enfolds in itself all whom he has won, binding itself in duty to them, and them reciprocally in duty to him (AB 121).

Note that the phrase in this passage points to the concreteness of the revelation of God in Christ, in terms of its impact on the present. Bonhoeffer's own elaboration of this is bold. He is daring to state the way in which this revelation *is!* It is not "back there" somewhere. If that were the case we could control it. It is here, where we are, in such a way that it can be seen. For it *is* the community.

The being of revelation does not lie in a unique occurrence of the past, in an entity which in principle is at my disposal and has no direct connection with my old or my new existence, neither can the being of revelation be conceived solely as the ever-free, pure and non-objective act which at certain times impinges on the existence of individuals. No, the being of revelation "is" the being of the community of persons, constituted and embraced by the person of Christ, wherein the individual finds himself to be already in his new existence (AB 123).

All of Bonhoeffer's later struggle with his own concept of reality lies between the lines in this interpretation of the phrase.

These passages offer clear indications of the way in which Bonhoeffer's concepts can be traced back to his earliest efforts at theological construction. More than this is needed, though, to authenticate the contention that what emerged after he got involved in the conspiracy has its origins in the initial efforts. What remains is the question of his creative attitude. In working out of the *Ethics*, as we have done, and in looking at the passages in *The Cost of Discipleship* on faith and obedience, we have encountered the formulations of an irrepressibly imaginative theologian. This, too, was present early. The idea of the analogy of relationship hardly comes from the mind of one who can only think others' thoughts after them. That concept was contained in the lectures on Genesis in the winter semester of 1932–1933. The same creativity is present in the lectures on Christology, given in the following session, the summer session of 1933. Here we are on thin ice, for we have only Bethge's reconstruction of these lectures from the notes of Bonhoeffer's students (though there is no question whatsoever as to the meticulous care that informs this reconstruction).

What arrests one's attention here is Bonhoeffer's treatment of the Chalcedonian formulation. At Chalcedon in A.D. 451 the great Christological controversies dominating the Church for better than a century and a half were brought to a settlement with the celebrated definition regarding the two natures of the one Jesus Christ.[8] Bonhoeffer referred to this as "the classic formulation of the doctrine of the God-manhood of Jesus Christ" (C 91), and commented on its significance in a way that manifests both his theological competence and his creative potential. As regards the former, he took the ground that any informed treatment must, namely, that the Chalcedonian formulation is more important for what it excludes than for what it says:

> What did the formula of Chalcedon say? It stated the *a priori* impossibility and impermissibility of taking the divinity and humanity in Jesus Christ side by side or together or as a relationship of objectifiable entities. Simple negations remain. No positive pattern of thought is left to explain what happens in the God-man Jesus Christ. Thus the mystery is left as a mystery and must be understood as such. Access is reserved solely for faith. All thought forms are cut short (C 91).

This is the fact that explains the curious way in which the decision at Chalcedon in the middle of the fifth century has both fascinated and plagued the Christian tradition ever since. What was fixed was a decision regarding the boundary conditions within which the understanding of the uniqueness and significance of Jesus Christ would continually strive for expression. The constructive question was focused by Chalcedon, but not answered, and all attempts to answer it would forever be tentative.

Bonhoeffer was acutely sensitive to this, and his insight pointed in a direction he would never desert, a direction that would tax his creative potential to the greatest extent.

> [The Chalcedonian definition] brings the concept of substance which underlies the relationship of the natures to a climax and does away with it. From now on it will no longer be permissible to say anything about the *substance* of Jesus Christ. Speculation about "natures" is at an end; the notion of substance is superseded. If a development of the Chalcedonian Definition were conceivable, it could not be a development in thought about the relationship of the natures; it would be something else which has still to be mentioned (C 92).

It would be utterly misleading to suggest that this insight provides all the impetus needed for an inexorable process of reflection yielding the ideas we have seen in the *Ethics*. More is needed than just the view that new concepts are always in order for the filling in of the middle of the Chalcedonian formula. What is needed is growth and stimulus, and these were to come in rapid and overwhelming tempo in the years ahead. At the same time, we have insisted that context alone is not enough to explain why Bonhoeffer came out where he did. It was not the conspiracy and imprisonment, it was not the agony of decision at Times Square, it was not the challenge and frustration of Finkenwalde, it was thoroughly rigorous wrestling with the sources of the Christian tradition that taught him that Chalcedonian Christology must be either open-ended or defective. And this he knew and stated conclusively in the passages before us from the lectures in the summer semester of 1933.

Suppose, now, that the further extension of the idea of "Christ existing as community," together with variations on this theme, was in fact the route along which Bonhoeffer moved in the search for that "something else which has still to be mentioned" that is always the moving horizon toward which Christology unfolds. This is not the only way to reflect on the development of Bonhoeffer's thought, especially given the incomplete and fragmentary character of his last writings. But it surely is one way to come to terms with the horizons he did see, providing that one is always chastened by the knowledge that no man's thought takes the shape for him that others see in the effort to move beyond him. Of course, what he had in mind when he used this phrase was the subsequent development of the lectures on which he was engaged, while we are deliberately expanding the phrase to embrace all that came later. We can do so in good conscience, however, for Christology was never absent from his thought, and what was present was a striking set of new reflections that suggest the way toward the future for any theology that gives Christology its rightful place. We can detect this both in the *Ethics* and in the *Letters and Papers from Prison,* and this is our purpose in the remainder of our discussion.

IV.

The Cutting Edge:
Context and Ethics

Much of the current conversation about Bonhoeffer's contribution to ongoing theological work is preoccupied with the letters from Tegel. This overlooks two decisive facts. The first is that the radical dimensions of his theology were already being sighted as he worked on his *Ethics*, specifically, in the section entitled "Thinking in Terms of Two Spheres." The second is that one of the most important things he wrote in the prison cell is published, not in the *Letters and Papers from Prison*, but as the last fragment in the *Ethics*, the discussion "What Is Meant by 'Telling the Truth'?" The first has to do with Bonhoeffer's most penetrating reflection about the Church in the midst of the context that is the modern world. The second contains his equally decisive insight into the nature of the Christian ethic. These two arguments constitute the cutting edge of his theology as it reached its culminating phases. If this is not understood, one cannot reckon at depth with what is going on in the *Letters and Papers from Prison*.

1. Thinking in Terms of Two Spheres

Bonhoeffer's rejection of "two-spheres thinking," as one must always put it after hearing his line of reasoning, is directly rooted in the christological concept of reality that we have now considered at length. (The argument we are going to analyze is the second of the three subsections making up his discussion of "Christ, Reality and Good.") One could simply treat this as his move beyond the limits of the classical Lutheran doctrine of the two kingdoms. Far more than this is at stake, however, for Bonhoeffer is here taking on what he had come to realize is *the* fallacy undermining much that has gone under the rubric of Christian ethics from the beginnings of the Christian tradition to the present. "Since the beginnings of Christian ethics after the times of the New Testament the main underlying conception in ethical thought, and the one which consciously or unconsciously has determined its whole course, has been the conception of a juxtaposition and conflict of two spheres, the one divine, holy, supernatural and Christian, and the other worldly, profane, natural and un-Christian" (E 196).

Obviously, in the light of all that we have heard Bonhoeffer say, he will counter such thinking at the very first remove. For it utterly misconceives the point of Christian ethics: "Reality as a whole now falls into two parts, and the concern of ethics is with the proper relation of these two parts to each other" (E 196). This can only fail in its very success, because it turns on the false assumption "that there are realities which lie outside the reality that is in Christ" (E 196). The only possible result of this is the illusion of the wrong dilemma. "So long as Christ and the world are conceived as two opposing and mutually repellent spheres, man will be left in the following dilemma: he abandons reality as a whole, and places himself in one or the other of the two spheres. He seeks Christ without the world, or he seeks the world without Christ. In either case he is deceiving himself" (E 197). Or, what is worse, this self-deception gives way to the attempt to stand in both spheres at once, the predicament of what Bonhoeffer calls "the man of eternal conflict" (E 197).

All this is familiar ground for us by now. Precisely these same points have been before us in other connections. A new note enters here, however. It is Bonhoeffer's attempt to clarify the relocation of the tension between the Christian and the world around him. If this must not be put in terms of two-spheres thinking, how can it be stated? Obviously, the matter

[81]

was crucial for him, for if two-spheres thinking cannot be overcome, and constructively replaced, then what was he doing as a Christian in the conspiracy?

The heart of the fallacy of two-spheres thinking is the "static antagonism" it continually yields. Bonhoeffer both described and then rejected this with great precision. The description runs this way: "Thought which is conducted in terms of two spheres regards such pairs of concepts as secular and Christian, natural and supernatural, profane and sacred, rational and revelational, as though they were ultimate static antitheses, serving to designate certain mutually exclusive entities" (E 198).

We must note very carefully the way in which this static antagonism was rejected. Bonhoeffer speaks of "the real concept of the secular," and we are already alert to the decisive overtone of the word "real" for him. We must also know that his word, *weltlich*[1] (literally: the "worldly") is properly rendered the "secular" in this phrase. The real concept of the secular, then—not the "secularism" that has so often given the term its negative connotation—has to do with the fact that that which is Christian can be found only in the world. Otherwise the basic claim of the Christian faith, arising from the reality of Christ, is denied. "It is now essential to the real concept of the secular that it shall always be seen in the movement of being accepted and becoming accepted by God in Christ. Just as in Christ the reality of God entered into the reality of the world, so, too, is that which is Christian to be found only in that which is of the world, the 'supernatural' only in the natural, the holy only in the profane, and the revelational only in the rational" (E 198).

All of the excitement that is generated by Bonhoeffer's creative flashes of insight in the closing years of his life is contained in a formulation like this one. The point is stated with a remarkable vigor and clarity while at the same time couched in some of the most cerebral theological terms. Hand in hand with this goes the staggering problem that leaps out of this way of putting the matter. One cannot help but note that the price to be paid for the insight is the grappling with the problem it yields. Just as some steal the insight by ignoring the problem, so others recoil from the problem and thus desert the insight. For Bonhoeffer there was only one way ahead. If the reality of God does enter the reality of the world in Jesus Christ, and if accordingly that which is Christian can be found only in the world, then the tension between Christ, and therefore the Christian, on the one hand, and the world, on the other, must be discerned in the midst of the world itself. It is the tension between the reality of Christ and the reality of the world apart from Christ.

Hence Bonhoeffer insisted immediately on the decisive emphasis, that "what is Christian is not identical with what is of the world. The natural is not identical with the supernatural or the revelational with the rational" (E 199). But how is this emphasis to be carried into a constructive alternative to two-spheres thinking? This is precisely the point to Bonhoeffer's argument, and his formulation contains one of his most important contributions to the theological work of the present day. (It should be noted well that his model for this striking assertion is Luther. It was classical Lutheranism, not Luther himself, that provided the clearest example of the two-spheres thinking he challenged.)

> Luther was protesting against a Christianity which was striving for independence and detaching itself from the reality in Christ. He protested with the help of the secular and in the name of a better Christianity. So, too, today, when Christianity is employed as a polemical weapon against the secular, this must be done in the name of a better secularity [*Weltlichkeit*] and above all it must not lead back to a static predominance of the spiritual sphere as an end in itself. It is only in this sense, as a polemical unity, that Luther's doctrine of the two kingdoms is to be accepted, and it was no doubt in this sense that it was originally intended (E 199).[2]

The better secularity—perhaps we should be more accurate and say "the better worldliness," for this is actually Bonhoeffer's own term. We do this not for pedantic reasons, nor do we mean to imply that the theology of secularization, so much before us recently, has no root in Bonhoeffer's thought in general and in this passage in particular. However, it is most important that later ideas not be read into Bonhoeffer's writings, especially at this juncture. For that can only blur the delineation of where Bonhoeffer himself was going and how far he moved. The problem of the *better worldliness* is the problem that supplants the fallacious question of how two spheres, one Christian and one unchristian, are to be related. Once this problem had taken the shape that it does here it never left Bonhoeffer's purview. It is fair to say that his thought both in the *Ethics* and in the *Letters and Papers from Prison* is preoccupied with it.

How so? How is it that he was preoccupied with the problem of the better worldliness from the time that he put it in the way we have just seen until the end? All his suggestions are tentative, of course, for he never had the opportunity to put his reflections into final form. What we have observed so far about the central role of Christology in his thought will remain, but always as the *living reality*, in his sense of the term, a reality that continually challenged him to move beyond the crystallization that now took form in his reflections. The truth is that Bonhoeffer could deal with the question of the better worldliness only by embarking on theological experimentation on a grand scale. This accounts in part for the broad diversity in the ways in which his findings have been utilized by others. When one observes the theological experiments of another he has his own in mind, and these will control what he sees.

The decisive insight reached in the section before us is contained in the passage we have noted. Bonhoeffer had more to say in this immediate context, and we must note two major points. In each of these we can observe the effect of the question of the better worldliness. What Bonhoeffer had done was to suggest the relocation of the tension between the Christian and the world in terms of an extremely dynamic frontier, and it is the *dynamic* character of this frontier, as over against the static antagonism that is the only possible result of two-spheres thinking, that he became so puzzled about, to the extent that his thought became restive beyond measure. In each of the two major implications he pressed in this immediate connection this is clearly evident.

(1) The first of these implications had to do with the Church and the world. The Church must not be reduced to "the status of a purely spiritual force" (E 201). This would be to deny the basic character of the Christian claim: "It is essential to the revelation of God in Jesus Christ that it occupies space within the world" (E 202). If this revelation does not occupy space it cannot be *real*. But can one talk about "space" this way without relapsing into two-spheres thinking? Bonhoeffer struggled with this with obvious discomfort. On the one hand, "The space of the Church is not there in order to try to deprive the world of a piece of its territory, but precisely in order to prove to the world that it is still the world, the world that is loved by God and reconciled with Him" (E 202). On the other hand, there is the drastic claim of the New Testament: ". . . it is implicit in the New Testament statement concerning the incarnation of God in Christ that all men are taken up, enclosed and borne within the body of Christ and that this is just what the congregation of the faithful are to make known to the world by their words and by their lives" (E 206). Hence, only a tension is discerned, one which must not be put in static, that is, spatial, terms: ". . . although the Church and the world are different from each other, yet there cannot be a static, spatial borderline between them. The question now is how one is to conceive this distinction between Church and world without relapsing into these spatial terms" (E 206–207).

The theologically puzzled Bonhoeffer of the closing years is clearly before us in this dilemma. The community of the faithful must *be*, and it must have *space*, or the faith is denied. But there cannot be a *spatial* borderline between it and the world, unless one is thinking about two spheres. What emerges, then, is a vexatious question. How does one get at the distinction between Church and world without thinking in terms of two spheres? This is the question. The issue is not "space"; it is, rather, the rejection of any notion of a *static* borderline between Church and world. This is why we have treated Bonhoeffer's struggle as having to do with the dynamic frontier between Church and world. It was with the dynamics of this frontier, not with mere metaphors, that Bonhoeffer was concerned in replacing two-spheres thinking with the search for the better worldliness. This discussion at hand turns on a precise formulation of this: "If one wishes to speak . . . of the space or sphere of the Church, one must bear in mind that the confines of this space are at every moment being overrun and broken down by the testimony of the Church to Jesus Christ" (E 293). Now, does this testimony ever overrun the confines of the space of the Church so completely that spatial metaphors are totally useless? Bonhoeffer's ultimate answer to this is ambiguous, as we shall see when we have the *Letters and Papers from Prison* before us.

(2) The second element in the search for the better worldliness had to do with the reverse side of the problem we have just noted. This is the question of the structure of life in the world, and it brings us to Bonhoeffer's concept of the *mandates*. This follows immediately on the heels of the reflections just examined (in the third and final subsection of "Christ, Reality and Good"). It is the direct extension of the argument at hand, and shows as clearly as any of the components of this argument what Bonhoeffer thought was the route to follow in the search for the better worldliness. When he put the question about how to distinguish between Church and world without relapsing into two-spheres thinking, Bonhoeffer simply asserted that we must go to the Bible for advice, and this advice he summed up as follows:

The world is relative to Christ, no matter whether it knows it or not. This relativeness of the world to Christ assumes concrete form in certain mandates of God in the world. The Scriptures name four such mandates: labour, marriage, government and the Church. We speak of divine mandates rather than of divine

[86]

orders because the word mandate refers more clearly to a divinely imposed task rather than to a determination of being (E 207).

Here Bonhoeffer is on very traditional ground, and his move beyond the limits of his heritage is subtle. One can discern what he is doing only by noting the import of his reason for the choice of the term "mandate." What lies behind this is his rejection of the time-honored concept of the "orders of creation." This classical concept has a long and tangled history as a theologically valid way of dealing with the world as it is apart from the revelation of God in Christ. This need not deter us here except in two respects. Theologically, the idea is debatable because it seems to speak of a significance that has nothing to do with Christ. Moreover, the concept utilized in this way had been ready at hand for those who sought a theological rationale for coming to some agreement with the Nazi state and thus it was immensely useful for the notorious cause of the German Christians. For the first of these reasons Bonhoeffer had rejected the concept as early as his lectures on Genesis in 1932–1933 suggesting in its place the concept of the "orders of preservation" (CF 88). And both of these factors are in play by the time he writes the passage now before us. By now even the notion of "orders" is too static. Hence the choice of the term "mandate" with its emphasis upon what man is to *do*.[3]

Bonhoeffer sought to permeate the whole understanding of the structure of life in the world with the same dynamic that informed his refusal to think in terms of two spheres. Thus the first three mandates—labor, marriage, government—are *not* to be juxtaposed with the fourth as worldly versus sacred. The point is not that the Church is worldly; it is, rather, that all *four* mandates are "divine" (thus this argument is of a piece with everything we have heard him say under the heading of "The Reality of Christ"): "[God] has not merely imposed one of these mandates on each individual, but He has imposed all four on all men. This means that there can be no retreating from 'secular' [*weltlichen*] into a 'spiritual' sphere. . . . And it will not do to regard the first three mandates as 'secular' [*weltlich*], in contradistinction to the fourth. For even in the midst of the world these are divine mandates" (E 207).[4] Moreover, Bonhoeffer's idea is thoroughly functional in its claim. It is the *task* of the mandates that is the clue to their being, not the reverse, and these tasks are meaningful only as the commands of God. "It is not because labour, marriage, government and church *are* that they are commanded by God, but it is because they are commanded by God that they *are*. And they are divine mandates only in so far as their being is consciously or unconsciously subordinated to the divinely imposed task" (E 208).

Such is the basic contention of Bonhoeffer's concept of the mandates. The *Ethics* abounds with extensions of it, sketches, actually, that paved the way for what he would say when the truly systematic writing of the work became possible. For our present purposes it will suffice to have dealt with this much, with the proviso that there is far more to see in the detail of the *Ethics* even as it stands. Two observations are in order before we move on. First, it is to be emphasized that Bonhoeffer developed this point *in the light of* the derivation of the question about the better worldliness. What is more, he never repudiated this way of setting out the groundwork for a fully developed Christian ethic. Both in the *Ethics* and in the *Letters and Papers from Prison* Bethge records the letter of January 23, 1944, in which this very concept of the mandates is briefly restated and extended (E 286–287; LP 102ff.). (Though one should take note of the fact that this letter is in advance of the letters in which the celebrated phrases from the prison correspondence appear.) Bonhoeffer is the hero and alleged prototype of many nihilists who perpetuate their own ignorance of his real (!) concern. He himself knew that where there is no sensitivity to the problem of structure there can be no ethic.

Second, it must not escape our notice that everything in Bonhoeffer's concept of the mandates depends on his understanding of the commandment of God. In a later section of the *Ethics* he took a major step from pious rhetoric to vigorous clarity as regards this point. "God's commandment, revealed in Jesus Christ, embraces the whole of life," he argued (E 280). If this is so, then it truly does have to do with life in all its vitality, and thus it must be as alive as the world is if two-spheres thinking and its accompanying abstractions are over-come in fact. Bonhoeffer did not shrink from this.

> The commandment of God becomes the element in which one lives without always being conscious of it, and, thus it implies freedom of movement and of action, freedom from fear of deci-sion, freedom from fear to act, it implies certainty, quietude, confidence, balance and peace. I honour my parents, I am faith-ful in marriage, I respect the lives and property of others, not because at the frontiers of my life there is a threatening "thou shalt not", but because I accept as holy institutions of God these realities, parents, marriage, life and property, which con-front me in the midst and in the fulness of life (E 280–281).[5]

What is more, once unleashed, the willingness to state the matter this clearly could not be stopped. Yet another of the very choice contributions of this figure to all who would match his rigorous reflection was the result: "The commandment of God is the permission to live as man before God. The com-mandment of God is permission. It differs from all human laws in that it commands freedom" (E 81). How free is the freedom the command of the real God commands? How free is the freedom of the man who is permitted to live as man be-fore God? In a moment we shall see.

"The Cutting Edge: Context and Ethics"—so we have titled this chapter. The point is now partially made. Bon-hoeffer could hardly have meant all that we claimed he meant under the rubric of "The Reality of Christ" if the question of the context were left in a secondary, insignificant place. No one can examine the passages we have without realizing this. The context is the world, and the world is alive. This offers a marvelous rule of thumb for the checking of any attempt to state the vast significance, the limitless reach, of God's mighty act in Jesus Christ. If a treatment of Christology does not incorporate the living world (to say nothing of the living God) it is *theologically* wrong. This is one of Bonhoeffer's most central findings, and it is intrinsic to the legacy he has left us. Its full import is only partially before us, though, for the depths of this insight have to do with the very nature of the Christian ethic itself. It too is alive.

2. What Is Meant by "Telling the Truth"?

What is the freedom that God commands? The section before us now is the place to look for the decisive clue to Bonhoeffer's ultimate answer. The test question for any worthy attempt at an ethic of any sort is always the question of truth. Bonhoeffer wrestled with this question in an absolutely unprecedented way.

As we noted in introducing this chapter, this is the terminal fragment in the *Ethics*. To be sure, it is to the *Ethics* that it belongs, rather than to the *Letters and Papers from Prison*. But this can mean that it is not known, or if known, then ignored, by those whose insight into Bonhoeffer's work is limited to the study of the *Letters* . . . alone. The importance of the fragment simply cannot be overstated. One could almost divide those who respond to Bonhoeffer's efforts into two camps—those who see this section as decisive, and those who, for any reason, do not.

The dating of the fragment is as much a clue to its importance as its content. As regards the content, *all* that we have seen thus far is in operation here. As regards the dating of it, note well the fact that it was written at Tegel. Unlike the rest of the *Ethics*, then, this piece was not developed during the time of the conspiracy. It reflects, rather, the days of the imprisonment, and the critical issue Bonhoeffer had to face from their outset. In the initial chapter of our discussion we saw that Bonhoeffer's imprisonment turned on that of Hans von Dohnanyi. In the long months of interrogation that followed the arrests, these two (plus Josef Müller) faced a common problem. The problem was how to avoid giving the Gestapo any indication of the conspiracy still hoping for success. (Their communication with each other was of course clandestine, and therefore severely limited.)[6] This they were able to do until all was lost with the failure of the plot on July 20 and the discovery of the Zossen papers in late September of 1944.

We have far more than brief intimations of the long cross-examination through which these men passed. Bethge sets this out with precise, meticulous care.[7] Early in this period of interrogation Bonhoeffer wrote the fragment. "What does it mean to tell the truth?" was not a theoretical problem for him when he worked out the insight the fragment contains. Of all the pieces he wrote in prison it is one of the clearest examples of the product yielded by the combination of his knowledge and ability with the demands of the context in which he was involved. What we have, then, is a priceless indication of the theological reflection that both informed and was informed by his concrete situation. In measuring it as of the utmost significance we are building on Bonhoeffer's own view. Bethge notes this. If these passages had been found they would have had a devastating effect on the case against Bonhoeffer. He saved them, however, and smuggled them out to his father after the events of July 20, 1944.[8]

Bonhoeffer began at the beginning, with the relationship between parent and child. "The truthfulness of a child towards his parents is essentially different from that of the parents towards the child." This led him to an immediate implication, "that 'telling the truth' means something different according to the particular situation in which one stands" (E 363). Given the talk about "situation ethics" these days, it might be wise to note that Bonhoeffer's word here is not "situation" (*Lage*) but "place" or "locality" (*Ort*).[9] The point is that telling the truth is a matter of a man's location, and for Bonhoeffer, this is a *relational* question. "The question must be asked whether and in what way a man is entitled to demand truthful speech of others. Speech between parents and child is, in the nature of the case, different from speech between

[91]

man and wife, between friends, between teacher and pupil, government and subject, friend and foe, and in each case the truth which this speech conveys is different" (E 363). Once he had said this Bonhoeffer moved directly to state the theological base of this contention: ". . . God is not a general principle, but the living God who has set me in a living life and who demands service of me in this living life" (E 364).

If Bonhoeffer is right, if, that is, the question of truth is a relational question (and one can trace his point all the way back to the analogy of relationship), then the fluid, living character of the truth that must be told is normative for the entire discussion. Bonhoeffer's way of insisting on this is striking just because it is both so succinct and so obvious. "Telling the truth is, therefore, something which must be learned. . . . the simple fact is that the ethical cannot be detached from reality, and consequently continual progress in learning to recognize reality is a necessary ingredient in ethical action" (E 364–365).[10] This has an immediate corollary, the idea of "living truth"—"If my utterance is to be truthful it must in each case be different according to whom I am addressing, who is questioning me, and what I am speaking about. The truthful word is not in itself a constant; it is as much alive as life itself" (E 365). Bonhoeffer rightly noted that this concept of living truth is dangerous. Well he might! But we will miss his deepest insight if we assume that what is at stake is simply the repetitious confrontation with his examiners at Tegel. For what is primarily involved is the living reality of God in Christ. This is always the overtone of his word "reality," as we well know. *This* reality *is* dangerous, for it demands a living response, and a living response is only there where the relational question is uppermost.

The thrust of the fragment is now before us. Bonhoeffer illustrated it with a memorable picture that can well serve as a paradigm or model for any serious attempt at a contextual ethic.[11] He moved into the illustration by way of an astute observation that only elaborates what we have already heard him say, but does so with all the warmth that any idea of *living* truth must have. "Every . . . word lives and has its home in a particular environment. . . . The word which has come to life in the warmth of a personal relationship is frozen to death in the cold air of public existence. . . . Each word must have its place and keep to it" (E 367). The illustration follows, the unforgettable picture of a little boy and a brutal teacher:

> When the various orders of life no longer respect one another, words become untrue. For example, a teacher asks a child in front of a class whether it is true that his father often comes home drunk. It is true, but the child denies it. The teacher's question has placed him in a situation for which he is not yet prepared. He feels that what is taking place is an unjustified interference in the order of the family and that he must oppose it. What goes on in the family is not for the ears of the class in school. The family has its own secret and must preserve it. The teacher has failed to respect the reality of this institution. The child ought now to find a way of answering which would comply with both the rule of the family and the rule of the school. But he is not yet able to do this. He lacks experience, knowledge, and the ability to express himself in the right way (E 367).

Living truth; truth, the telling of which must be learned— everyman can find himself in this picture. Everyman is therefore vulnerable to its impact. "The child's answer can indeed be called a lie; yet this lie contains more truth, that is to say, it is more in accordance with reality than would have been the case if the child had betrayed his father's weakness in front of the class" (E 368).

Memorable though this is in its own right, we cite it in detail mainly in order to put before us in all its relentless logic *the* insight for which this fragment is the vehicle. This is Bonhoeffer's radical, stark juxtaposition of the *truth* of Satan with the *truth* of God. It lies at the key turning point of the discussion, preparing the way for the statement of the concept of living truth. "It is only the cynic who claims 'to speak the truth' at all times and in all places to all men in the same way . . ." (E 365). He is known by the fact that he "destroys the living truth between men" (E 366). Flesh and blood is on this in the figure of the teacher in the picture. It is the cynic who gives concreteness to "the truth of Satan."

> Its essence is that under the semblance of truth it denies everything that is real. It lives upon hatred of the real and of the world which is created and loved by God. It pretends to be executing the judgement of God upon the fall of the real. God's truth judges created things out of love, and Satan's truth judges them out of envy and hatred. God's truth has become flesh in the world and is alive in the real, but Satan's truth is the death of all reality (E 366).

Bonhoeffer knew who the enemy is. He is the cynic. This obtains in the illustration, and it surely manifested itself in the only days he would know from this time until his execution. The concept of living truth is derived from the concept of reality and is thus at the center of Bonhoeffer's thought. Its great power is not just that it clarifies the contextual nature of the Christian ethic, for it yields far more than this. Bonhoeffer's version of such an ethic is not normless! It recognizes the real in the living. It discerns the truth of Satan in the cynic. It serves the reality of the living. It combats the hatred of reality in the cynic. How free is the man who is given permission to live as man before God? He is free to struggle for reality against the cynic.

Even more than the concept of the mandates, this underscores the move beyond the static borderline that is the only frontier two-spheres thinking can discern. We have heard him say that "the ethical cannot be detached from reality" and that ethical action is accordingly rooted in the unfolding of "learning to recognize reality" (E 364–365). What is the freedom that God commands? It is the freedom to recognize reality in the search for the better worldliness. The Tegel correspondence must be read in this light.

V.

The Far Horizons

The phrases by which Bonhoeffer is best known come from the *Letters and Papers from Prison*. We have purposely not dealt with them yet, alluding to them only occasionally in the course of our considerations. It is all too easy to read them back into the material we have had before us, and thus to fail to do the reverse, namely, ponder their meaning against the background of Bonhoeffer's thought as it had taken shape earlier. The *Letters* are indeed memorable as they stand, but their real force is to be apprehended only if one has an awareness of Bonhoeffer's earlier discussions, and the direction in which he was already moving before his arrest. This is the first point we must make in approaching the *Letters*. It has informed our entire discussion.

A second, equally important point must be known by any who would deal significantly with the *Letters*. This has to do with the immediate limitations on Bonhoeffer's work in prison. It is probably self-evident, and for that reason alone must be emphasized, for in theological discussions the self-evident is often overlooked. In the cell at Tegel (and of course this is even more the case regarding the few items from the time after Tegel), Bonhoeffer labored without the tools of his trade. Bethge tells us that all he had with him as he worked out the letters were his German Bible, a Greek New Testament, and a concordance. Thus, his reflections on the biblical text were not informed by lexicons or commentaries, save as he could remember them. Moreover, his voracious reading followed a pattern one might not expect. For one thing, he obviously did not keep many books with him (indeed, they served as a vehicle for messages to the outside). But far more significant than that, he did not work primarily with theology. His concern was, rather, with so-called secular literature— novels, philosophy, history—and this primarily from the nineteenth century, both because the prison authorities would not permit access to the immediately contemporary, and because his theological concerns were now driving him to broad cultural studies.[1]

Taken together, these two points establish the perspective for our discussion. There is a lot that is new in the *Letters*. We have already noted Bethge's remark that the correspondence was "Bonhoeffer's elixir of life in Tegel." [2] He actually did more than simply break new theological trails, and the serious student of Bonhoeffer will not wish to miss a single word. For our purposes here, though, we must content ourselves with his specifically theological reflections. In the light of all that we have been wrestling with, it must be clear that Bonhoeffer labored to carry forward the reflections already under way. He was busy shaping the new questions that now burst on the far horizons for him, hoping one day to work on them with all the apparatus theology requires.

Now this surely should not surprise us. It is, in fact, the way theology is done. New questions are continually being generated by any theology worthy of the name, and they result in fresh examination of the sources and the new context for ways of expression that point to new insights. In this sense, the *Letters* carry on a process long under way. *Ethics* has insights *The Cost of Discipleship* does not. *The Cost of Discipleship* is beyond the lectures at Berlin. And these lectures are surely beyond *The Communion of Saints* and *Act and Being*. The progression this flashback suggests is anything but neat. No line of reflection, in theology or anything else, is devoid of its unexpected moments. But it will help us to unlock the secrets of the mighty phrases of the *Letters* if we know that what Bonhoeffer is doing is formulating the leading questions for future work, and setting out tentative answers to be tested and developed later. To be sure, some of these suggested answers already contain gigantic, bold conclusions, and it is our task

to discern these. But the result will more often be the fur-
rowed brow. Indeed, the promise of Bonhoeffer is caught up
with just these questions, and it is as yet unfulfilled.

In this connection Bethge's observation is acute. All things
considered—especially including the pattern of Bonhoeffer's
reading and the nature of his prior work—"What came forward in 1944 in new delineations of the question [*Fragestel-
lung*] came less from theological publications than from Bonhoeffer's experience in the military courts, the context of the
cell, and his involvement with secular [*säkularen*] literature." [3]

The pivotal juncture for our concerns here is the letter to
Bethge of April 30, 1944. Bonhoeffer now began the process
of shaping the questions that have assured him forever a place
in the purview of theology as it unfolds in the second half
of our century. From the process begun in this letter and
continued until Bonhoeffer was taken from Tegel to Prinz-
Albrecht-Strasse there emerge three astonishing phrases, with
which we must now struggle.

1. The World Come of Age

We may discuss this idea properly only if we know that the
emphasis must fall on its fluidity and movement. Bonhoeffer
had several ways of phrasing it, all with different combinations
of the same words, but the fact is that the wording which yields
translations such as the "world which has become of age" or
"world which is becoming of age" is far more frequent than
that behind "come of age world." [4] Moreover, in some contexts it does indeed make sense for the phrase to be translated
"the adulthood of the world." To be sure, the phrase that
can be literally translated "world come of age" (*die mündige
Welt*) does occur, in the letter of July 18, 1944. [5] But even
here one should be very clear regarding just the words themselves. John Godsey, who wrote the first full-length study of
Bonhoeffer in English, has pointed to this in a recent article
on "Reading Bonhoeffer in English Translation: Some Diffi-

culties" (an article to be commended to any reader of this present discussion). Godsey insists that we "remember that the word *'mündig'* in German refers to that time when a young person turns twenty-one and not to the adult maturity of the wise old sage!" [6]

The idea first comes up in the letter of June 8, 1944. Now we have noted that Bonhoeffer embarked on new theological construction at the end of April, and we shall be returning to the letter in a moment. In the letter of June 8, he was extending his efforts by way of responding to questions from Bethge, and it is here that the idea of the world come of age came into play. Note carefully how it does: "I will try to define my position from the historical angle" (LP 167).[7] From the historical angle, then—for the idea is strictly an attempt to epitomize the modern context historically understood—Bonhoeffer argues as follows:

> The movement that began about the thirteenth century (I am not going to get involved in any argument about the exact date) towards the autonomy of man (in which I should include the discovery of the laws by which the world lives and deals with itself in science, social and political matters, art, ethics and religion) has in our time reached an undoubted completion. Man has learnt to deal with himself in all questions of importance without recourse to the "working hypothesis" called "God" (LP 167–168).

We must not move too quickly to Bonhoeffer's point about the working-hypothesis-God, for more is needed to deal with this, and presently we shall have the issue in front of us in sharp focus. For the moment the crucial thing to notice is that, in his characterization of the autonomy of man, Bonhoeffer includes "religion." So that when he says "everything" in the following lines he really means it. He means *everything including religion.* ". . . it is becoming evident that everything gets along without 'God'—and, in fact, just as well as before. As in the scientific field, so in human affairs generally, 'God' is being pushed more and more out of life, losing more and more ground" (LP 168).

[98]

What was particularly aggravating to Bonhoeffer, that phase of the situation to which he was most sensitive, was the manner in which Christians have characteristically reacted to this. For Christians have characteristically treated it as a "great defection," with the inevitable result that "the development considers itself to be anti-Christian." The immediate setting of Bonhoeffer's introduction of the idea of the world come of age is his depicting of the prevalent stance of Christian apologetics in the face of this modern temperament.

> Christian apologetic has taken the most varied forms of opposition to this self-assurance. Efforts are made to prove to a world thus come of age that it cannot live without the tutelage of "God." Even though there has been surrender on all secular [*weltlichen*] problems, there still remain the so-called "ultimate questions"—death, guilt—to which only "God" can give an answer, and because of which we need God and the Church and the pastor (LP 168).[8]

This stance Bonhoeffer regarded to be utterly reprehensible, even loathsome. It both besmirches the reality of Christ and insults the integrity of man. It is, in fact, senseless!

> The attack by Christian apologetic on the adulthood of the world [*die Mündigkeit der Welt*] I consider to be in the first place pointless, in the second place ignoble, and in the third place unchristian. Pointless, because it seems to me like an attempt to put a grown-up man back into adolescence, i.e. to make him dependent on things on which he is, in fact, no longer dependent, and thrusting him into problems that are, in fact, no longer problems to him. Ignoble, because it amounts to an attempt to exploit man's weakness for purposes that are alien to him and to which he has not freely assented. Unchristian, because it confuses Christ with one particular stage in man's religiousness, i.e. with a human law (LP 169).[9]

What is more, such a characteristic reaction of Christians to the world come of age misses the decisive question completely. The issue is that this development, far from being the occasion for defensive action on the part of Christians, is actually the opening for a stunning, new articulation of what the Christian faith is all about. For the world come of age should be better understood in the light of Christ than in its own light! "Thus the world's coming of age is no longer an occasion for polemics and apologetics, but is now really better understood than it understands itself, namely on the basis of the gospel and in the light of Christ" (LP 172).

If one knows the point to Bonhoeffer's rejection of two-spheres thinking, then it is obvious that that argument and this one must be read together. In two respects the question of rejecting two-spheres thinking has been carried further. When Bonhoeffer launched the earlier argument he spoke of the fallacious question as having prevailed "Since the beginnings of Christian ethics after the times of the New Testament" (E 196). The point was in part historical in character, and clearly it is here too. Only now it is stated more precisely. What Bonhoeffer is talking about, in a word, is the deep contrast between the modern and the medieval worlds. Christendom, medieval Christian civilization, both in its Catholic and in its Protestant forms, is now gone. And with its disappearance has gone the place of God, Church, and pastor, as either Catholic or Protestant theology in the thought world of the medieval frame of reference put it. Any refusal to recognize this is a refusal to recognize where man now is. Bonhoeffer's idea of the world come of age vividly captures this. The world come of age is the world beyond Christendom —it is our world.[10]

There is a second respect in which the argument rejecting two-spheres thinking is sharpened by the idea of the world come of age. In this new connection, as well as in the earlier one, *the* question at hand is the christological question. The letter of June 8 is an explicit indication of this. The point is even more clearly argued in the letter of the following June 30. An apologetic that insists on the wrong questions simply runs out of creativity. When man is honest, and therefore will not admit its first moves, then a total, unresolvable impasse results. The moves of theology in this key are complicated indeed, for, as Bonhoeffer sees it, what happens is that theology leaves the issue of God to the realm of "the so-called ultimate questions" and takes over the arguments of "existentialist philosophy and psychotherapy" in order to bludgeon man into a sense of need he does not have. The point to the maneuver is that "this man can now be claimed for God." But what if he refuses the cogency of the argument? ". . . if he cannot be brought to see and admit that his happiness is really an evil, his health sickness, and his vigour despair, the theologian is at his wit's end" (LP 179). This brings the real burden of Bonhoeffer's indictment into view. The impasse is wrong, not only because it denies a world come of age, but also because what has been overlooked is the very heart of the faith.

> You see, that is the attitude that I am contending against. When Jesus blessed sinners, they were real sinners, but Jesus did not make everyone a sinner first. He called them away from their sin, not into their sin. It is true that encounter with Jesus meant the reversal of all human values. So it was in the conversion of Paul, though in his case the encounter with Jesus preceded the realization of sin. It is true that Jesus cared about people on the fringe of human society, such as harlots and tax-collectors, but never about them alone, for he sought to care about man as such. Never did he question a man's health, vigour, or happiness, regarded in themselves, or regard them as evil fruits; else why should he heal the sick and restore strength to the weak? Jesus claims for himself and the Kingdom of God the whole of human life in all its manifestations (LP 179–180).

Hence, the new question: "Let me just summarize briefly what I am concerned about—how to claim for Jesus Christ a world that has come of age" (LP 180).

The question is *in part only* an unanswered question for Bonhoeffer. It is so customary to emphasize the fragmentary character of his prison writings that one can eventually get the idea that he had not reached *any* conclusions. This is wide of the mark—drastically so—for it mistakes the significance of what was going on in the cell at Tegel. Of course Bonhoeffer had unfinished business to do. What theologian does not! St. Thomas's *Summa Theologica* was unfinished, so was

Barth's *Church Dogmatics* (and he was emphatically on record that it never would be finished). One would hardly misconstrue the unfinished business there. Why then with Bonhoeffer? This is the most pernicious form of the disease that infects all who treat the work of a martyr. The fact of the martyrdom, and hence the interrupted character of the work, can blind one. The death of any young creative person, martyr or not, can blind one. To see in the idea of the world come of age *only* a question is to allow yearning for knowledge of what might have been to replace insight into what in fact was. This would be like asking to hear what Mozart would have composed had he lived into his seventies and never really listening to the magnificence of what he did leave us.

Without doubt the question of claiming for Jesus Christ a world come of age is open-ended. But to put the question this way represents also the beginnings of an answer. This is always true in the reflective disciplines at large, and it is particularly true of theology. The formation of new questions includes at least the groundwork of the subsequent reflection. And even more than that is present in the idea of the world come of age. For Bonhoeffer now knew that the search for the better worldliness entailed a deep commitment—an irrevocable one—to *all* that makes the modern world modern. What Bethge has taught us to understand as the transition from Christian to contemporary yielded a theological insight that, to be sure, others have shared. But it also yielded an epitomizing concept that is unique to Bonhoeffer, an idea that is bold and suggestive in a way seldom if ever rivaled. The idea of a world come of age as *Christ's* world is one of the choicest fruits of his theological labors.

2. Nonreligious Interpretation

The second great idea from the Tegel correspondence is the idea of the "non-religious interpretation of theological concepts," and its counterpart, the idea of "religionless Christianity." Here too there is a variety of phraseology. The former is by far the more frequent, as Bethge succinctly indicates: "Bonhoeffer himself used the term 'religionless Christianity' only in the first theological letter from Tegel, April 30, 1944 (twice there), i.e., just when starting his new approach. The phrase used in all the following letters is 'non-religious interpretation' or some closely connected derivative (about eleven times)."[11] The fact is that both emphases are present in Bonhoeffer's idea, and only together do they display what he meant to indicate.[12] For our purposes the decisive examples occur in the letter of April 30, where this line of reflection came to the surface, and in the letter of June 8, where it is found in close proximity with the introduction of the idea of the world come of age.

We must state the point of the concept in its various forms at the outset. The world come of age is the world beyond religion—it is not the world beyond Christ. How can the world come of age be claimed for Jesus Christ? That is, what has the gospel of Christ to do with the *modern* world? Whatever it has to do with the world come of age, it cannot have to do with religion. If that is so, then the standard move of Christianity for the two millennia of its existence must be rejected, and the question is: What takes the place of this standard maneuver? For Bonhoeffer this was a double-edged question: What, really, is Christianity for us today? *Who*, really, is Christ for us today? All this seethes in Bonhoeffer's introduction of the idea at hand. Note carefully by way of examining the first passage that by "religionless" he means to convey his appraisal of the concrete reality of the present: words (whether they be theological or pious), inwardness, conscience—these comprise religion-in-general for him, and they no longer speak.

> You would be surprised, and perhaps even worried, by my theological thoughts and the conclusions that they lead to. . . . What is bothering me incessantly is the question what Christianity really is, or indeed who Christ really is, for us today. The time when people could be told everything by means of words,

whether theological or pious, is over, and so is the time of inwardness and conscience—and that means the time of religion in general. We are moving towards a completely religionless time; people as they are now simply cannot be religious any more (LP 139).

Now what if it is a fact that man's religious propensity (technically referred to as the "religious *a priori*") is in fact historically conditioned? That would seem to be what is now clear. What, then, does that do to Christianity?

Our whole nineteen-hundred-year-old Christian preaching and theology rest on the "religious *a priori*" of mankind. "Christianity" has always been a form—perhaps the true form—of "religion". But if one day it becomes clear that this *a priori* does not exist at all, but was a historically conditioned and transient form of human self-expression, and if therefore man becomes radically religionless—and I think that that is already more or less the case (else how is it, for example, that this war, in contrast to all previous ones, is not calling forth any "religious" reaction?)—what does that mean for "Christianity"? (LP 139–140).

If the ancient faith in the Christ makes any sense at all, then it must transcend the limits of any historically conditioned epoch. That has its converse implication: If the ancient faith in the Christ makes any sense at all, then it too is historically conditioned (it has to do with *reality*), for it can transcend the limits of a given epoch's mood by becoming relevant to a new context and its concerns. All that we saw under the rubric of "The Reality of Christ" demands this. In the Tegel correspondence Bonhoeffer was delineating the new leading questions that were direct extensions of his conviction concerning the living reality that is the Christ. We have shown that the idea of the world come of age contains both a searching question and the beginnings of a penetrating answer. The same is true here. Bonhoeffer moved in two steps. The first was to put the question: What is religionless Christianity?

. . . if our final judgment must be that the western form of Christianity, too, was only a preliminary stage to a complete absence of religion, what kind of situation emerges for us, for the Church? How can Christ become the Lord of the religionless as well? Are there religionless Christians? If religion is only a garment of Christianity—and even this garment has looked very different at different times—then what is a religionless Christianity? (LP 140).

The second step was to refine this question in terms of a sharper formulation of it. Here again we must note that the word translated "secular" is "*weltlich*," and should be read "worldly." [13]

What do a church, a community, a sermon, a liturgy, a Christian life mean in a religionless world? How do we speak of God —without religion, i.e. without the temporally conditioned presuppositions of metaphysics, inwardness, and so on? How do we speak (or perhaps we cannot now even "speak" as we used to) in a "secular" way about "God"? In what way are we "religion-less-secular" Christians, in what way are we the *ekklesia*, those who are called forth, not regarding ourselves from a religious point of view as specially favoured, but rather as belonging wholly to the world? (LP 140–141).

The refinement of the question implies the beginnings of an answer, and it certainly contains unshakable conclusions already reached. Bonhoeffer had a lot going for him when he began to break a new trail in the letter of April 30. Hence it is not at all unfair to put a broad construction on the question just noted. Indeed, if the question is read without any awareness of the background yielding it, an irresponsible display of culpable ignorance is the only possible result, especially when this happens on the part of those who are theologically informed. Bonhoeffer wondered about how we can speak of "God" (the quotes are in the German text too[14])—that is, the God, not of religion, but the God who is *real* in Jesus Christ. How can we speak of "God," seeing that we are who we are, namely religionless-worldly Christians, and seeing that there is only one way for such people to speak—a worldly way?

[105]

Thus, the question from the letter of April 30 is: How do we speak as religionless-worldly Christians in a worldly way about "God"?

There are three decisive implications of this question that manifest just how clearly Bonhoeffer knew that the issue's open-ended character is itself dependent on specific conclusions.

(1) Bonhoeffer was clear on what he meant by the *religion* he was rejecting. He meant *metaphysics* and *inwardness*, and specifically said so in the passages we have just had before us. Christianity can no longer thrive on speculative hypotheses about ultimate truths that cannot be seen. There is, of course, far more than this to "metaphysics," as every beginning philosophy student knows full well. No reflective conversation can be as self-contained or as self-evident as those who live by cursing the term "metaphysics" are always trying to suggest. At the same time it is not totally without merit that the whole idea of metaphysics is severely in doubt these days, and from so many different quarters. And as far as Bonhoeffer was concerned, when speculation takes over for concreteness in Christian thought, *religion* is perpetuated in a way that man in a world come of age simply cannot abide. The same goes for *inwardness*, which always thrives on individualism. After all, how can any man really understand the inwardness of another? The *Letters* abound, as do all of Bonhoeffer's writings, with deep, meditative reflection, but concreteness, people, reality, always punctuate this reflection. One could hardly construe Bonhoeffer as a proponent of the kind of mysticism that is connoted by the term "inwardness" in his searching question. So understood, religion—i.e., metaphysics and inwardness—is out. The point is of a piece with what we have already watched him work out with reference to the Church in the *Ethics*. It is impossible to imagine Bonhoeffer ever deserting this conclusion.

(2) Bonhoeffer was likewise clear on what the question, as refined, implied for theological work. It implied the task of developing the "non-religious interpretation of theological

concepts." (We will locate the phrase in context in a moment.) Obviously, *religion* and *theology* are antithetical here. The striking thing is the way the phrase comes up. If the time of religionless Christianity is here, then nonreligious theology must unfold. Thus the question at hand generates a new task.

The phrase is a direct application of the idea of religionless Christianity. In this new form it received its decisive use in Bonhoeffer's brief critical remarks about the theologians he knew as older contemporaries. The remarks are brief, of necessity, but the fact that they are present at all is of far greater significance than might be supposed. It is part of the genius of German theology that theological creativity must clear its point of departure in differentiation from what everyone else is thinking. This is where the scientific character of German theology originates. We will always be studying the Germans because they do in the open and with precision what everyone else in the trade does but often does not admit. This leads to all kinds of cultural blind spots—to German arrogance in this as in all fields (and Bonhoeffer's Prussian being could be as insufferable in this as anyone's!), as well as to the caricatures of those whose own chauvinism is the cover for indolence. However all that may be, Bonhoeffer was clear on where he stood on the matter at hand as over against others. Troeltsch was admired because at least he took the issue seriously. Tillich, with his attempt to rehabilitate the word "religion," was just turning the clock backwards. Bultmann made a great stride, but did not go far enough, and thus landed in the trap of typical liberal reductionism. And Barth saw the issue clearly—more so than anyone else—but, having seen it, was all the more culpable for not taking seriously his own leads. All this (and he names others) is said in the letter of June 8, and some of it is said in the letter of May 5, and those who are interested in the details can easily find them (cf. LP 170–172 and 143–145 respectively). A full-blown systematic discussion would demand that these points be made with depth and precision, and there can be little doubt that this is what

[107]

Bonhoeffer would have picked up had he survived. *This* is the heart of the unfinished business of the idea!

Fortunately for us, he was most precise in his critique of Barth, probably because he was closer to Barth of all the people he named, and had been most influenced by Barth's work. This is the setting of the new version of the idea (he had just referred to Troeltsch, Heim, Althaus, and Tillich):

> Barth was the first to realize the mistake that all these attempts (which were all, in fact, still sailing, though unintentionally, in the channel of liberal theology) were making in leaving clear a space for religion in the world or against the world. He brought in against religion the God of Jesus Christ, *"pneuma* against *sarx".* That remains his greatest service (his *Epistle to the Romans,* second edition, in spite of all the neo-Kantian egg-shells). Through his later dogmatics, he enabled the Church to effect this distinction, in principle, all along the line. It was not in ethics, as is often said, that he subsequently failed—his ethical observations, as far as they exist, are just as important as his dogmatic ones—; it was that in the non-religious interpretation of theological concepts he gave no concrete guidance, either in dogmatics or in ethics. There lies his limitation and because of it his theology of revelation has become positivist, a "positivism of revelation", as I put it (LP 170–171).

The bite to this critique depends on what Bonhoeffer meant by "positivism of revelation," and more than that, this will offer us the major clue as to what he meant by nonreligious interpretation of theological concepts. He had made a remark in the letter of May 5 on which the passage we have just noted is dependent:

> Barth was the first theologian to begin the criticism of religion, and that remains his really great merit; but he put in its place a positivist doctrine of revelation which says, in effect, "Like it or lump it": virgin birth, Trinity, or anything else; each is an equally significant and necessary part of the whole, which must simply be swallowed as a whole or not at all. That is not biblical (LP 144).

[108]

No such positivism may be countenanced, not if we are to think through theology in a nonreligious way. Why? Here the deep root of Bonhoeffer's training at the hand of Seeberg prevails. As we noted at the outset of Chapter II, Seeberg had taught Bonhoeffer that the traditional headings of theological reflection are arbitrary. One can utilize them, but one need not. The difference between Bonhoeffer and Barth is that Bonhoeffer knew this and Barth did not. The implication of the critique is gigantic. Even the *structure* of theology must be redone if it is to be of any use for a religionless Christianity. To be sure, Barth's *Church Dogmatics* had effected radical changes in the structure of theology and Bonhoeffer knew of them. But the effect of Barth's efforts has been to intensify the "take-it-or-leave-it" character of theology which can only make sense where some traces of the Christian *religion* linger on.

Were he still with us, Bonhoeffer would be the first to protest that this critique of Barth, and the remarks regarding the others as well, are hardly the last words on the matter at hand. A quarter of a century has passed since the Tegel letters were written. In 1944, Troeltsch was in a state of eclipse even for Bonhoeffer, Tillich had yet to write his *Systematic Theology*, Bultmann's mighty contribution was just beginning to crystallize, and Barth's *Church Dogmatics* had eight layers yet to go (III/1 through IV/2, Second Half). Bonhoeffer's critiques remain trenchant, however, and must be taken seriously even in the light of subsequent developments, as we shall be saying in the concluding chapter.

(3) Bonhoeffer was also clear on the *theological* character of the task of nonreligious interpretation. Religion is dead but "God" is not, not for Bonhoeffer, and those who adduce his support in this bizarre claim simply have not read him. The point is explicit in the letter of July 16, which contains the Latin phrase, *etsi deus non daretur* that Bonhoeffer translates "even if there were no God"—*auch wenn es keinen Gott gäbe* (LP 186).[15] The passage in question is absolutely crucial for discerning Bonhoeffer's far horizons, for it brings together

both the idea of nonreligious interpretation and the idea of the world come of age. "I am only gradually working my way to the nonreligious interpretation of biblical concepts . . . ," he began. He proceeded to the historical question again, and brought the noted Latin phrase into play. He referred to several dimensions of the cultural situation, the most succinct of which concerned the natural sciences and the idea of the infinite universe. The point is that the universe so conceived is "self-subsisting, *etsi deus non daretur*" (LP 187). Here as elsewhere, the concept of God is not needed for the development of the ideas whereby man understands his context in every respect. The working-hypothesis-God is as dead as a doornail. "God as a working hypothesis in morals, politics, or science, has been surmounted and abolished; and the same thing has happened in philosophy and religion (Feuerbach!). For the sake of intellectual honesty, that working hypothesis should be dropped, or as far as possible eliminated" (LP 187).

But the working-hypothesis-God is not the God of the Bible, and here honesty and theological insight coincide exactly. They do so in such a way that once this is seen one can never speak of God as if he were the needed working hypothesis without denying the God of whom the Bible speaks. Or more importantly, the discarding of the God of religion becomes the necessary presupposition for any authentic speaking of the God who is real in Christ. These lines include the decisive formulation we must never overlook: *Vor und mit Gott leben wir ohne Gott* ("Before and with God we live without God").[16] It is totally wrong to observe only the last four words. Bonhoeffer did not separate his sentence. Neither dare we, or anyone who cites them.

> . . . we cannot be honest unless we recognize that we have to live in the world *etsi deus non daretur*. And this is just what we do recognize—before God! God himself compels us to recognize it. So our coming of age [*Mündigwerden*] leads us to a true recognition of our situation before God. God would have us know that we must live as men who manage our lives without him. The God who is with us is the God who forsakes us (Mark

15.34). The God who lets us live in the world without the working hypothesis of God is the God before whom we stand continually. Before God and with God we live without God. God lets himself be pushed out of the world on to the cross. He is weak and powerless in the world, and that is precisely the way, the only way, in which he is with us and helps us. Matt. 8.17 makes it quite clear that Christ helps us, not by virtue of his omnipotence, but by virtue of his weakness and suffering (LP 188).

If there is any paragraph in the whole of Bonhoeffer's writings that must be known and cited in its entirety or not at all, this is it. It contains his most radical theological insight, without any qualification whatsoever. And it sounds boldly new. It should not, for it is as old as the gospel that informs all his thought!

Taken together, the ideas of the world come of age and the nonreligious interpretation point to the task Bonhoeffer discerned as *the* task now before theology. Clearly, this is a powerful extension of the christological theme that has been with us all along. Christology in a new, though ancient, key becomes the starting point for the work of "worldly interpretation."

. . . we may say that the development towards the world's coming of age outlined above, which has done away with a false conception of God, opens up a way of seeing the God of the Bible, who wins power and space in the world by his weakness. This will probably be the starting-point for our "secular interpretation" [*weltliche Interpretation*] (LP 188).[17]

3. The Secret Discipline

Twice in the *Letters* Bonhoeffer used a cryptic word—*Arkandisziplin*, "secret discipline." Neither he nor his horizons are before us until we have come to terms with this word, and its rare occurrence almost assures its being missed. Bethge rightly places it alongside the two ideas we have just considered as indicative of the task toward which theology must proceed if Bonhoeffer's work was correct.[18] Paul Lehmann, in his article "Faith and Worldliness in Bonhoeffer's Thought," also focuses attention on this crucial word.[19] In citing the views of these two we are building on the insights of two of the theologians who have taken both the man and his work most seriously.

Surely one can hardly know the life and thought of Bonhoeffer without being impressed by the discipline of spirit that marked it. The two major works from the Finkenwalde days give memorable expression to this, *The Cost of Discipleship*, which we have pondered, and *Life Together*, which we have not. The rationale for leaving the latter on the table can now be made explicit. The fact is that both Bonhoeffer's theology and his involvement brought him far beyond its confines. The ordering of the life of Finkenwalde, however, bears witness to the sense of discipline that carried him through Tegel to the gallows, and it should be commended as the background for the question that now came before him.

The word first arose in the letter of April 30 in close connection with the idea of religionless Christianity. We have heard him ask, How do we speak in a worldly way about "God"? And we have heard him wonder how religionless-worldly Christians are to regard themselves as the Church given wholly to the world. If these questions are cogent, then ". . . Christ is no longer an object of religion, but something quite different, really the Lord of the world. But what does that mean? What is the place of worship and prayer in a religionless situation? Does the *secret discipline* . . . take on a new importance here?" (LP 141, italics added).

The passage containing the second occurrence of the word has also been before us in part. This is in the letter of May 5, and it is part and parcel of Bonhoeffer's critique of Barth's take-it-or-leave-it theology. Here we need the whole passage again in order to see what Bonhoeffer is suggesting. Considered from the angle of the question just noted, the trouble with all-or-nothing theology is that it makes the question of discipline too easy! If one can just buy the whole package, then the question of discipline is already solved. Bonhoeffer's astonishing suggestion is that this *profanes* the mysteries of the Christian faith.

> Barth was the first theologian to begin the criticism of religion, and that remains his really great merit; but he put in its place a positivist doctrine of revelation which says, in effect, "Like it or lump it": virgin birth, Trinity, or anything else; each is an equally significant and necessary part of the whole, which must simply be swallowed as a whole or not at all. That is not biblical. There are degrees of knowledge and degrees of significance; that means that *a secret discipline* must be restored whereby the *mysteries* of the Christian faith are protected against profanation. The positivism of revelation makes it too easy for itself, by setting up, as it does in the last analysis, a law of faith . . . (LP 144, italics of the phrase added).

We have argued above that Bonhoeffer's understanding of the nonreligious interpretation was *theological* in character, and in that connection we have insisted that the line, "Before and with God we live without God," must remain intact or be misused. This is the clue to the secret discipline. The life of worship and prayer does not disappear. It is just that it is no longer evident in itself. The life before God is known as a life *before God* only by the believers themselves. Thus, in a world come of age the life of the Christian before God is a matter of *secret* discipline, a discipline that in itself the world may well not see. All the world can behold by its own lights are the results!

One must read the *Letters* as a whole to appreciate this fully. For the *Letters* manifest not only the theological frontiers we have been examining but also the life of obedient faith and faithful obedience of which they are the expression. This will be seen in the constant devotional use to which Bonhoeffer put the Bible he had with him. It will also be seen in the poetry he attempted (and which we have studiously avoided, for the poems should be read in their entirety in the exact contexts in which they occur).

In the idea of the secret discipline, Bonhoeffer was commencing new exploration into the doctrine of the Church. Without the community of faith, the identity of Christians in the midst of the world come of age will be overcome by the identification of the same Christians with the same world. This is Lehmann's point: ". . . for Bonhoeffer, the discipline of faith is necessary to keep identification of the Christian with the world from swallowing up his identity." [20] And Bethge says the same thing in a different way. He is struck by the fact that Bonhoeffer's idea of the secret discipline has its only point in what we have called the search for the better worldliness, and it is at the same time that which alone can maintain the integrity of this search. "The secret discipline without worldliness is a ghetto; worldliness without the secret discipline is only a boulevard." He goes on to argue that the former alone winds up in the mind-set of the monk, while nonreligious interpretation by itself becomes merely an intellectual game.[21]

The issue is hardly minimal. It points to the source of strength that Bonhoeffer's theological explorations, to say nothing of his life, presupposed. At the same time it exposes the risks that his work must generate for those who respond to what he attempted with similar efforts. All kinds of impetuous maneuvering can claim Bonhoeffer's support. It is entirely possible to be gripped by the drama of this man's life and the boldness of his thought, and go racing off to plot against the nearest leader at hand on the grounds that all tyrants (or supposed tyrants) are to be dispatched in the name of the better worldliness. Likewise, it is entirely possible to be stunned by the boldness of his thought and the drama of his life and assume on that ground that man *is in control* of the subject matter of theology, and that the efforts of yesterday are to be held up to derision in the name of a wiser tomorrow. Neither move, let alone their combination, points to the realization of the promise of Bonhoeffer. For both overlook the demands of the secret discipline. How free is the man who is permitted to live as man before God? We have asked this before. He is free to recognize reality in the search for the better worldliness. So we began to answer. Now we must add even more to the qualitative note. Such a search can be carried on only by the secretly disciplined, those whose identity stems from the life before God. Only such can discover the promise of Bonhoeffer.

VI.

The Promise

The significance of the fact that the man we are dealing with died nearly a quarter of a century ago may well have struck the reader already. If not, let it strike him now. Bonhoeffer is the symbol and personification of avant-garde theology. He should not be. We should be beyond him. Until we are, the promise of this man will not have been realized.

Twenty-five years is the twinkling of an eye, of course, when it comes to the ongoing development of Christian thought. Bonhoeffer's thought has been before us for years now, but what we have not had until these present days is the detailed story of Dietrich Bonhoeffer himself. So what we have all had to put up with has been a plaster saint, either one's own or someone else's, and the creation of plaster saints has undermined more theology in the wild history of the Christian tradition than a dozen books could list. The appearance of Bethge's magnificent biography has ended this once and for all. The plaster saint has been replaced by a real man, with all the limits of all men of either high or low ability. We can grapple with Bonhoeffer now. We do not have to guess about him any more. Therefore we can proceed to the task of second guessing his ideas. For the only point to thinking his thoughts after him is to think these thoughts beyond him.

Thinking Bonhoeffer's thoughts beyond him is both a dangerous and a fascinating task. It is dangerous because the process will always sound as though it is making the claim that had Bonhoeffer lived he would have come out where we do. He who would work with Bonhoeffer's ideas has no choice but to run this risk, with a huge disclaimer stated at the outset. The disclaimer is the denunciation of any and all who argue

from another's martyrdom to the cogency of their own conclusions. And this disclaimer can be authenticated only by
grounding one's appropriation of Bonhoeffer's concepts in the
study of his life and thought *as a whole*. We have barely
scratched the surface in this connection here, but one can at
least hope that by ranging across the spectrum of his theology
with close attention to the events in the midst of which he
worked, the possibility that others will see different things in
him is nourished, not hidden. However that may be, it should
be clear by now that building theologically on the *Letters*
alone is categorically indefensible.

Thinking Bonhoeffer's thoughts beyond him is not only
dangerous, however. It is also fascinating. When one works
up through his ideas, it is impossible to arrest the momentum
and stop where he had to. Considered in the broader context
of the theological milieu of which he is a part, he emerges as
a decisive transitional figure, pointing toward a new phase of
theological work in the modern time. As the liberal theology
that trained him was giving way before a radical shift in perspective and method just when he was taking up his tasks, so
it can and must be said that that second phase of Protestant
theology in the modern world now seems to shudder under the
impact of an equally decisive shift in the goal and perspective
of theological work. And in this day of new relationships
across the old divide, the impact of Bonhoeffer's work is
hardly confinable to Protestant circles alone, for increasingly
some Catholics and some Protestants know a common brotherhood around new theological problems that can never be dis-
placed. This fascinating task of theology in a new key awaits
all who work through this man in order to work beyond him.

The subject of the conversation about Bonhoeffer could
take up a small book in itself. In a way, the point of this
present discussion has been to prepare the reader both for his
own study of Bonhoeffer's works and for his own critical
dialogue with books about him. One will quickly see in operation the cardinal rule we are suggesting. Discussions that
adduce Bonhoeffer in support of fragmentary theology as an

end in itself, and that develop this argument with *pieces* of the *Letters*, are obviously wrong in the light of what we have seen. Moreover, the conversation *about* Bonhoeffer is really not as important as the use to which his insights are being put in works that listen authentically to him and then go their own independent way toward the horizons he was one of the first to sight. Paul Lehmann's *Ethics in a Christian Context* (1963) is at the head of this list. Arend van Leeuwen's *Christianity in World History* (1964) is close behind. And the conversations about *hope* as the decisively central category for new theological construction—Jürgen Moltmann's *Theology of Hope* (1964; English translation, 1967) and Dietrich Ritschl's *Memory and Hope* (1967)[1]—surely receive new cogency if one approaches them with a knowledge of Bonhoeffer. This brief listing is suggestive, not exhaustive, for Bonhoeffer is already a figure who cannot be ignored, but it may serve as an extension of a remark that Bethge makes late in the biography. He notes that when the *Letters* first appeared in print the time was not ripe for Bonhoeffer to get his own hearing. The great debate between the Bultmannians and the Barthians was in full swing, and insofar as Bonhoeffer's ideas figured in this at all, they did so inside the points of view of the proponents of one or the other side.[2] And the case could be made either way. That debate was never really resolved and is now largely spent. The fact is that the questions Bonhoeffer was wrestling with drive beyond the limits of each of these monumental positions.

From the perspective of our discussion, the promise of Bonhoeffer's theology has to do with the development of what might be called *ethical theology*. Twice we have explicitly spoken of this (see pp. 53–54 and 68, above) though it has been with us throughout the whole of our reflections. This is where Bonhoeffer was going. If he was as correct as the present writer is persuaded, then there is no choice but to continue on. An *ethical theology* has to do with neither the replacement of theology by ethics nor the absolutizing of the social-action syndrome. It involves, rather, the ethical intensification of *all* theological concepts. This alone responds to and corresponds with the task of claiming for the Christ a world come of age and the task of discerning in the world come of age the reality of the Christ who is the Lord. It is the way in which obedient faith and faithful obedience thinks about the reality of Christ in a world come of age. All the rich treasury of Christian thought, from (and including) the Bible forward, must be re-thought with this in mind. This is what Bonhoeffer was actually doing, and we have been watching him. But his own argument has rightly commanded our attention as we have reflected on what he has said. What if our argument were to assume control? How would he sound then? How do we put him to work *now* in the development of an ethical theology? This is properly the subject for another discussion. Here only a brief indication is in order. Two passages may help us see what is involved.

(1) When Bonhoeffer first put the question about the secret discipline, he related it to a pivotal idea that had emerged in the *Ethics*. Yet once more we must back up to fill in a deliberate omission. The full question reads as follows: "What is the place of worship and prayer in a religionless situation? Does the secret discipline, or alternatively the difference (which I have suggested to you before) between penultimate and ultimate take on a new importance here?" (LP 141; cf. E 120ff.).

Penultimate and ultimate: Actually the distinction is between "the last things and the things before the last" (*die Unterscheidung . . . von Vorletztem und Letztem*[3]). In the religionless situation this distinction leaps to life. An ethical theology concentrates on the pressure on today of the imminent tomorrows—not the distant tomorrows, but the ones close in, in which the God who is real in Jesus Christ is immanent. This is where God is, in the world come of age as it moves on toward its imminent tomorrows. The God who is real in Jesus Christ is on the move, then. He truly transcends us, for our tomorrows are filled with only one certainty, namely, that he will be there. To discern him one must look

not "up" but "forward." Obedient faith and faithful obedience knows that our todays always stand under the sign of the
resurrection. For the today that was Good Friday could not
contain the God who there in his weakness drew near to man,
so that man even in torment could be before him.

To discern the God who is real in Jesus Christ in the mist
of the fast-approaching tomorrows is an ethical task. Concreteness, earthiness, humanity are its mark, and his. This is
why no man can hear the gospel of Christ except through the
events that conspire to constitute his own time. The theme of
the ethics of the reality of Christ is therefore always comprised of the search for an ever-renewing fulfillment. The
Kingdom of God is always at hand. An ethically presented
eschatology replaces a mystical one. For the fulfillment of the
purposes of the God who is real in Jesus Christ coincides with
the liberation of the men who are commanded to be free
before him.

(2) The letter of August 3, 1944, has been before us. It
contains the remark concerning "modern" and liberal theology
which we found useful in suggesting the twin sources of Bonhoeffer's theological creativity. As we noted, that letter contains the "Outline for a Book" that Bonhoeffer never had a
chance to finish. Here there are not even the somewhat
finished fragments that we are accustomed to handling by now.
Here there are only brief sketches—broad brush strokes that
have only begun to cling to the canvas. Consider the following:

Who is God? Not in the first place an abstract belief in God,
in his omnipotence, etc. That is not a genuine experience of
God, but a partial extension of the world. Encounter with
Jesus Christ. The experience that a transformation of all human
life is given in the fact that "Jesus is there only for others." His
"being there for others," maintained till death, that is the
ground of his omnipotence, omniscience, and omnipresence.
Faith is the participation in this being of Jesus (incarnation,
cross, and resurrection). Our relation to God is not a "religious"
relationship to the highest, most powerful, and best Being imag-
inable—that is not authentic transcendence—but our relation

to God is a new life in "existence for others," through participation in the being of Jesus. The transcendental is not infinite and unattainable tasks, but the neighbour who is within reach in any given situation. God in human form—not, as in oriental religions, in animal form, monstrous, chaotic, remote, and terrifying, nor in the conceptual forms of the absolute, metaphysical, infinite, etc., nor yet in the Greek divine-human form of "man in himself," but "the man for others," and therefore the Crucified, the man who lives out of the transcendent (LP 202).

Bethge notes that these lines contain "a new Christological title for Bonhoeffer." [4] The one who discloses reality is "the man for others." This captures the ethical impact of the heart of the Christian faith—the Christ himself. *Only* vis-à-vis others can he be discerned at all. The Christology of an ethical theology must regard this as *the* all-embracing fact.

In its own way the "Outline for a Book" symbolizes the promise of Bonhoeffer. We must fill it out on our own, not worrying about how he might have done it, but rejoicing, rather, in the task that we can carry forward because of his prior effort. Dietrich Bonhoeffer served *the* man for others by becoming *a* man for others. So must we all, for we too have a promise to share.

Notes

Chapter I. The Man

1. Eberhard Bethge, *Dietrich Bonhoeffer* (München: Chr. Kaiser Verlag, 1967), p. 381. (All following references to this work will be abbreviated "Bethge, DB" followed by the page number.)
2. Bethge, DB, p. 430.
3. Bethge, DB, p. 485.
4. A detailed account may be found in William L. Shirer, *The Rise and Fall of the Third Reich* (New York: Simon and Schuster, 1960), pp. 314ff.
5. Bethge, DB, pp. 702–704.
6. Bethge, DB, p. 702, my translation.
7. Bethge, DB, p. 700.
8. *The Way to Freedom*, letters, lectures and notes, 1935–1939, from the *Collected Works* of Dietrich Bonhoeffer, Vol. II, edited and introduced by Edwin H. Robertson, translated by Edwin H. Robertson and John Bowden (New York: Harper & Row, 1966), p. 246. Cf. also Dietrich Bonhoeffer, *Gesammelte Schriften*, herausgegeben von Eberhard Bethge (München: Chr. Kaiser Verlag, 1958), Vol. I, p. 320. And Bethge, DB, p. 736.
9. Bethge, DB, pp. 765ff.
10. Cf. Bethge, DB, pp. 759–760.
11. Cf. Bethge, DB, pp. 850–866. For Bishop Bell's account, cf. *I Knew Dietrich Bonhoeffer*, edited by Wolf-Dieter Zimmermann and Ronald Gregor Smith, translated from the German by Käthe Gregor Smith (London: Collins, 1966), pp. 196–211. This translation of *Begegnungen mit Dietrich Bonhoeffer: Ein Almanach* (München: Chr. Kaiser Verlag, 1964) is a marvelous compendium of impressions of the man.
12. A portrayal of this remarkable woman by Werner Koch may be found in *I Knew Dietrich Bonhoeffer*, pp. 114ff.
13. Maria von Wedemeyer-Weller, "The Other Letters from Prison," in *Bonhoeffer in a World Come of Age*, edited by Peter Vorkink, II (Philadelphia: Fortress Press, Paperback Edition, 1968), p. 104. (Subsequent references to this very helpful collection of articles that originally appeared in the Fall, 1967, issue of the *Union Seminary Quarterly Review* [Vol. XXIII, No. 1] will be abbreviated BWCA.)
14. Cf. Bethge, DB, pp. 873ff., and 877ff. For William Shirer's account, cf. Shirer, *op. cit.*, pp. 1018ff. (though his contention on pp. 1017–1018 that Bonhoeffer's disclosure of the names of the conspiracy to Bishop Bell led to his and others' execution must surely be challenged as completely erroneous).
15. Bethge, DB, p. 940.
16. Maria von Wedemeyer-Weller, *op. cit.*, BWCA, pp. 103–113.
17. Dietrich Bonhoeffer, *Ethics*, edited by Eberhard Bethge, translated

by Neville Horton Smith (New York: The Macmillan Company, paperback edition, 1965; this edition follows the order of the sixth German edition [München: Chr. Kaiser Verlag, 1963]), p. 11.

18. Bethge, "Turning Points in Bonhoeffer's Life and Thought," in BWCA, p. 78.

19. *Ibid.*, pp. 78–79.

20. In contrast with Barth, who was a preacher who became a theologian, as Bethge observes, DB, p. 223.

21. Cf. Paul Lehmann, "Faith and Worldliness in Bonhoeffer's Thought," in BWCA, pp. 44–45. We will deal with this matter in some detail in the third section of Chapter V.

22. Bethge, DB, p. 760.

23. Cf. Bethge, in BWCA, pp. 73–78, and Lehmann, in BWCA, pp. 25–27.

24. Lehmann, in BWCA, p. 25.

25. Bethge, DB, p. 890. I have directly paraphrased his statements.

26. Bethge, in BWCA, p. 87; cf. DB, pp. 284, 893. (The passage in question is found in Bonhoeffer, *Gesammelte Schriften*, Vol. IV, p. 71.)

27. Bethge, DB, p. 762.

28. Bethge, DB, p. 955; cf. Otto Dudzus, in *I Knew Dietrich Bonhoeffer*, p. 82, who remembers a more graphic version of the remark, though it is not supported by direct citation.

Chapter II. Conclusions along the Way

1. Bethge, DB, p. 99.
2. Cf. Bethge, DB, pp. 216–228.
3. Bethge, in BWCA, p. 86.
4. Bonhoeffer, *Schöpfung und Fall*, Theologische Auslegung von Genesis 1 bis 3 (Dritte Auflage; München: Chr. Kaiser Verlag, 1955), p. 7, my translation.
5. Cf. *ibid.*, p. 43, for Bonhoeffer's own phrase.
6. Bethge, in BWCA, pp. 78–79, 85–86.
7. John Godsey, in his very helpful article, "Reading Bonhoeffer in English Translation: Some Difficulties" (BWCA, pp. 114–131), calls attention to the fact that Bonhoeffer's own division of the book was twofold, rather than the four chapters of the English translation. He sets out this twofold organization in detail (BWCA, pp. 118–120).
8. Quoted by Bethge, in BWCA, p. 181.
9. Cf. *Nachfolge* (Sechste Auflage; München: Chr. Kaiser Verlag, 1958), p. 3: Bonhoeffer's last sentence reads "Teure Gnade ist Menschwerdung Gottes." Thus, "Costly grace is God's becoming man." To be sure, *Menschwerdung* means "incarnation"; even so, the German term "says" more than the stylized English theological equivalent. This point should be observed whenever the term "incarnation" appears in the translations.
10. *Nachfolge*, p. 19.

Chapter III. The Reality of Christ

1. Cf. *Ethik* (Sechste Auflage; München: Chr. Kaiser Verlag, 1963), p. 29: Bonhoeffer's word, "Begegnung," should be translated "encounter," as we have done, rather than "meeting" as in the translation.

2. *Ethik*, p. 208.

3. *Ethik*, p. 206.

4. Such as John Godsey, *The Theology of Dietrich Bonhoeffer* (Philadelphia: Westminster Press, 1960), the first major treatment of Bonhoeffer's thought in English, and John A. Phillips, *Christ for Us in the Theology of Dietrich Bonhoeffer* (New York: Harper & Row, 1967; published in England under the title *The Form of Christ in the World*).

5. *Sanctorum Communio*, Theologische Bücherei, Neudrucke und Berichte aus dem 20. Jahrhundert, Band 3, Systematische Theologie (München: Chr. Kaiser Verlag, 1954), p. 145.

6. Bethge, in BWCA, p. 66; cf. also Godsey, in BWCA, p. 123.

7. I have dealt extensively with the thought of Ernst Troeltsch in my *Toward a Theology of Involvement* (Philadelphia: Westminster Press, 1966). Accordingly, the question of the relationship between Troeltsch and Bonhoeffer is particularly fascinating for me. The fact that Bonhoeffer did not come to terms with Troeltsch's thought in the dissertation can be shown conclusively. This demonstration, though germane, would take us into a prolonged discussion that would be out of place here.

8. Cf. Henry Bettenson, *Documents of the Christian Church* (New York & London: Oxford University Press, 1947), pp. 72–73, and John H. Leith, *Creeds of the Churches* (Garden City, N.Y.: Doubleday, Anchor Books, 1963), pp. 34–36, for translations of the Chalcedonian Definition. Leith gives a brief introduction and some bibliographical suggestions.

Chapter IV. The Cutting Edge: Context and Ethics

1. *Ethik*, p. 211.

2. *Ethik*, p. 212.

3. Cf. in this connection the later passages in *Ethics*, pp. 287–288.

4. *Ethik*, p. 220.

5. Because we have made so much of Bonhoeffer's concept of reality, it should be pointed out that the word here translated "realities" is *Gegebenheiten* rather than his usual *Wirklichkeit* (cf. *Ethik*, p. 297). Thus here these are "givens" rather than "realities."

6. Cf. Bethge, DB, p. 912, for details.

7. Cf. Bethge, DB: regarding von Dohnanyi, pp. 898ff.; regarding Bonhoeffer, pp. 910ff.

8. Bethge, DB, p. 914.

9. *Ethik*, p. 385.

10. Bonhoeffer's word *Erkennenlernen* should be rendered by the phrase "learning to recognize" rather than the phrase "learning to appreciate," as it stands in the translation. This is so crucial that I have translated it this way in the passage.

11. This entire fragment is of decisive significance for Paul Lehmann's *Ethics in a Christian Context* (New York: Harper & Row, 1963).

Chapter V. The Far Horizons

1. Bethge, DB, p. 945; also Bethge's marvelous list of Bonhoeffer's readings while in Tegel, DB, pp. 1102–1104.
2. Bethge, DB, p. 940.
3. Bethge, DB, p. 946.
4. Bethge makes this point in "Bonhoeffer's Christology and his 'Religionless Christianity'" (in BWCA, pp. 56–57). He makes the same point in the biography, and those who can handle German will find this latter statement more helpful, since he includes the references to the German text that demonstrate the point: DB, p. 972, notes 172 and 173.
5. *Widerstand und Ergebung* (Neunte Auflage; München: Chr. Kaiser Verlag, 1959), p. 246; cf. LP 191.
6. John Godsey, in BWCA, p. 123.
7. As we begin detailed discussion of passages from the *Letters and Papers from Prison*, attention must be called to the chaos of editions through which the English translation has passed. Happily, we now have the carefully revised, and at many points that means drastically corrected, translation cited here: the third edition, revised and enlarged, of 1967 (SCM Press Ltd., London, and The Macmillan Company, New York). We are following this translation throughout our discussion, utilizing the paperback edition (Macmillan). John Godsey, in the article noted above (n. 6), deals in detail with this problem (BWCA, pp. 123ff.). I can only concur with his conclusion that all editions of the translation prior to the 1967 edition should be burned!
8. *Widerstand und Ergebung*, p. 216.
9. *Widerstand und Ergebung*, p. 217.
10. Bonhoeffer's precursor here was Troeltsch, who demonstrated massively the point Bonhoeffer's idea epitomizes, as I indicate in my *Toward a Theology of Involvement*. Bonhoeffer himself was at least partially aware of this in the letter before us; cf. LP 170.
11. Bethge, in BWCA, pp. 46–47, n. 1.
12. This is clearly noted in the essay noted above (n. 11). It is given a more emphatic articulation in the biography, DB, p. 977.
13. *Widerstand und Ergebung*, p. 180.
14. *Ibid.*
15. *Ibid.*, p. 240.
16. *Ibid.*, p. 241.
17. *Ibid.*, p. 242.
18. Bethge, DB, pp. 988ff.
19. Lehmann, in BWCA, pp. 41ff. Lehmann notes (p. 42, n. 21) the most significant discussion at depth of this so far to appear, the essay by Gisela Meuss in Vol. III of *Die Mündige Welt* (pp. 68–115), "Arkandisziplin und Weltlichkeit bei Dietrich Bonhoeffer."

20. Lehmann, in BWCA, p. 44.
21. Bethge, DB, p. 992.

Chapter VI. The Promise

1. In 1959 Moltmann published a study of Bonhoeffer (*Herrschaft Christi und soziale Wirklichkeit nach Dietrich Bonhoeffer*); this now appears in English translation in *Two Studies in the Theology of Bonhoeffer*, by Jürgen Moltmann and Jürgen Weissbach, introduction by Reginald H. Fuller, translated by Reginald H. Fuller and Ilse Fuller (New York: Charles Scribner's Sons, 1967). This is not the only source of the insights he develops in *Theology of Hope*, translated by James W. Leitch (New York: Harper & Row, 1967), but it is certainly one of them. Dietrich Ritschl, in his *Memory and Hope* (New York: The Macmillan Company, 1967) makes frequent reference to Bonhoeffer.

2. Cf. Bethge, DB, pp. 998–1000, for his own way of stating this.
3. *Widerstand und Ergebung*, p. 180.
4. Bethge, in BWCA, p. 69.

Bibliography

The Works of Bonhoeffer
in English Translation

(Insofar as possible these are listed in the order in which Bonhoeffer wrote them.)

The Communion of Saints. Translated by Ronald Gregor Smith and others. New York: Harper & Row, 1963. British edition entitled *Sanctorum Communio.* London: William Collins Sons, 1963.

Act and Being. Translated by Bernard Noble with an introduction by Ernst Wolf. New York: Harper & Row, 1962.

"Concerning the Christian Idea of God," *The Journal of Religion,* Vol. XII, No. 2 (April, 1932), pp. 177–185.

Godsey, John D., *Preface to Bonhoeffer:* The Man and Two of His Shorter Writings. Philadelphia: Fortress Press, 1965. Contains: "Thy Kingdom Come" (written in November, 1932); "The First Table of the Ten Commandments" (written during the summer of 1944).

Creation and Fall. Translated by John C. Fletcher. New York: The Macmillan Company, 1959; paperback edition, 1965 (includes *Temptation*).

Christ the Center. Translated by John Bowden with an introduction by Edwin H. Robertson. New York: Harper & Row, 1966. British edition entitled *Christology.* London: William Collins Sons, 1966.

The Cost of Discipleship. Translated by Reginald H. Fuller with a memoir by G. Leibholz. New York: The Macmillan Company, first edition, abridged, 1948; second edition, unabridged and revised, 1959; paperback edition, 1963.

Temptation. Translated by Kathleen Downham. New York: The Macmillan Company, 1955; paperback edition, 1965 (includes *Creation and Fall*).

Life Together. Translated with an introduction by John W. Doberstein. New York: Harper & Row, 1954.

Selected translations from Bonhoeffer's collected writings. (Source: *Gesammelte Schriften.* Edited by Eberhard Bethge. 4 volumes. München: Chr. Kaiser Verlag, 1958–1961):

   No Rusty Swords: Letters, Lectures and Notes, 1928–1936, from the *Collected Works* of Dietrich Bonhoeffer, Volume I. Translated by by Edwin H. Robertson and John Bowden. Edited with an introduction by Edwin H. Robertson. New York: Harper & Row, 1965.

   The Way to Freedom: Letters, Lectures and Notes, 1935–1939, from the *Collected Works* of Dietrich Bonhoeffer, Volume II. Translated by Edwin H. Robertson and John Bowden. Edited with an introduction by Edwin H. Robertson. New York: Harper & Row, 1967.

Ethics. Edited by Eberhard Bethge. Translated by Neville Horton Smith. New York: The Macmillan Company, 1955; paperback edition (following the order of the sixth German edition), 1965.
Letters and Papers from Prison. Edited by Eberhard Bethge. Translated by Reginald H. Fuller. London: SCM Press, first edition, 1953; second edition revised, 1956. American edition entitled *Prisoner for God.* New York: The Macmillan Company, 1954; paperback edition entitled *Letters and Papers from Prison,* 1962; third edition, revised and enlarged, New York: The Macmillan Company, 1967; paperback edition, 1967.
I Loved This People. Translated by Keith R. Crim with an introduction by Hans Rothfels. Richmond: John Knox Press, 1965.

Major Secondary Sources

Bethge, Eberhard. *Dietrich Bonhoeffer:* Theologe, Christ, Zeitgenosse. München: Chr. Kaiser Verlag, 1967. (An English translation is in preparation.)
Bonhoeffer in a World Come of Age. Edited by Peter Vorkink, II, with a foreword by John C. Bennett. Essays by Paul M. Van Buren, Paul L. Lehmann, Eberhard Bethge, Maria von Wedemeyer-Weller, and John D. Godsey. Philadelphia: Fortress Press, 1968.
Godsey, John D. *Preface to Bonhoeffer:* The Man and Two of His Shorter Writings. Philadelphia: Fortress Press, 1965.
————. *The Theology of Dietrich Bonhoeffer.* Philadelphia: Westminster Press, 1960.
I Knew Dietrich Bonhoeffer. Edited by Wolf-Dieter Zimmermann and Ronald Gregor Smith. Translated by Käthe Gregor Smith. Foreword by W. A. Visser 't Hooft. New York: Harper & Row, 1967.
Moltmann, Jürgen. "The Lordship of Christ and Human Society," in *Two Studies in the Theology of Bonhoeffer,* by Jürgen Moltmann and Jürgen Weissbach. Introduction by Reginald H. Fuller. Translated by Reginald H. Fuller and Ilse Fuller. New York: Charles Scribner's Sons, 1967.
Phillips, John A. *Christ for Us in the Theology of Dietrich Bonhoeffer.* New York: Harper & Row, 1967. British edition entitled *The Form of Christ in the World.* London: William Collins Sons, 1967.
The Place of Bonhoeffer: Problems and Possibilities in His Thought. Edited and introduced by Martin E. Marty. Essays by Peter Berger, George Forell, Reginald Fuller, Walter Harrelson, Franklin Littell, Jaroslav Pelikan, and Franklin Sherman. New York: Association Press, 1962.
World Come of Age. Edited with an introduction by Ronald Gregor Smith. Essays by Karl Barth, Eberhard Bethge, Rudolf Bultmann, William Hamilton, Hanfried Müller, Regin Prenter, and Hans Schmidt. Philadelphia: Fortress Press, 1967.

(Excellent bibliographies of articles, essays, and related works may be found in *Bonhoeffer in a World Come of Age,* pp. 135–140, by Peter Vorkink, II, and in *Preface to Bonhoeffer,* pp. 70–73, by John D. Godsey.)